IXL SUMMER WORKBOOK

THE ULTIMATE SUMMER WORKBOOK

FOR THE SUMMER BETWEEN GRADES 2 & 3

© 2025 IXL Learning. All rights reserved. No part of this publication may be reproduced, stored in a retrieval system, or transmitted, in any form or by any means (electronic, mechanical, photocopying, recording, or otherwise) without the prior written permission of IXL Learning.

ISBN: 978-1-964670-05-8
29 28 27 26 25 1 2 3 4 5

Printed in the USA

About this book

Keep your child engaged with learning over summer break with the Ultimate IXL Summer Workbook! The activities in this workbook are perfect for reinforcing key skills from the past year and building new skills in preparation for the year ahead.

DAILY PRACTICE

This workbook contains 60 days of activities. Each day consists of 2 full pages of activities that can be completed in about 15 minutes. At 5 days per week, this workbook is perfect for a 12-week summer break! Throughout the week, your child will engage in math and language arts activities, complete a science or social studies page, and wrap up with enrichment activities.

BRAIN BREAKS

Brain breaks are sprinkled throughout. These fun breaks include physical and sensory activities.

ACTIVITY TRACKER

Track your child's progress with the activity tracker! Have your child color in the bubble or cover it with a sticker after completing each day's work. Watch as the tracker fills up throughout the summer!

CERTIFICATE OF COMPLETION

Found at the back of the book, the certificate of completion is a great way to help you recognize your child's hard work!

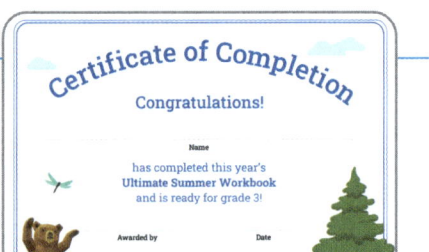

 **Materials:** To complete this workbook, your child will need a pencil and crayons or colored pencils.

Continue the fun with IXL.com!

Throughout the book, look for these IXL.com skill IDs. For additional practice, go to the website or the IXL mobile app and enter the three-digit code into the search bar.

IXL.com skill ID
JJX

IXL provides all the tools your child needs to succeed.

LIMITLESS LEARNING

Unlock your child's full potential with access to 17,000 engaging units in math, English, science, social studies, and Spanish. With examples and 1,300 video lessons across all grade levels, your learner can review a concept before diving into a skill.

PERSONALIZED PLAN

IXL's Diagnostic pinpoints your child's knowledge level and creates a customized plan to boost achievement.

REAL-TIME FEEDBACK

Detailed explanations after missed questions allow your child to learn from mistakes and work toward achieving mastery.

AWARDS AND CERTIFICATES

Whimsical awards and certificates help you celebrate your child and keep motivation high.

EDUCATIONAL GAMES

Fun-filled games provide hands-on practice in essential concepts and help your child develop a love of learning.

20% off For a limited time, receive 20% off your IXL family membership. Visit **www.ixl.com/workbook/23s** or scan the **QR code** for details.

© IXL Learning

Activity tracker

Keep track of your progress! Color in the bubble or cover it with a sticker after you complete each day's work.

Week 1 Days 1–5	1	2	3	4	5
Week 2 Days 6–10	6	7	8	9	10
Week 3 Days 11–15	11	12	13	14	15
Week 4 Days 16–20	16	17	18	19	20
Week 5 Days 21–25	21	22	23	24	25
Week 6 Days 26–30	26	27	28	29	30
Week 7 Days 31–35	31	32	33	34	35
Week 8 Days 36–40	36	37	38	39	40
Week 9 Days 41–45	41	42	43	44	45
Week 10 Days 46–50	46	47	48	49	50
Week 11 Days 51–55	51	52	53	54	55
Week 12 Days 56–60	56	57	58	59	60

Weeks 1–3: Overview

Week 1

Math
Place value
Addition and subtraction within 20

Language arts
Synonyms
Cause and effect
Short and long vowel sounds

Science
States of matter

Enrichment
Sudoku
Word scramble

Week 2

Math
Two-digit addition and subtraction
Comparing numbers

Language arts
Consonant blends
Capitalization
Sequence of events

Social studies
Urban, suburban, rural

Enrichment
Riddles
Logic puzzle

Week 3

Math
Three-digit addition and subtraction
Telling time

Language arts
Antonyms
Consonant digraphs
Fact or opinion

Science
Natural resources

Enrichment
Word categories
Scavenger hunt

More ways to learn

Keep the learning going! Summer is the perfect time to explore, learn, and have fun. Use these simple, exciting activities to help you stay active, curious, and creative during your summer break.

See how many activities you can do! Cross off each activity as you complete it.

Set up a relay race to run with friends. 	**Find a new recipe and give it a try.** 	**Play a board game.** 
Start a journal to record your summer adventures. 	**Pack a meal or snacks and have a picnic outside.** 	**Write a letter to a friend.** 
Make your name out of things you find on a nature walk. 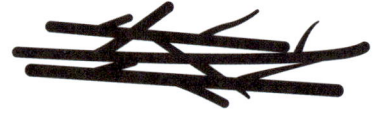	**Start a garden.** 	**Make puppets out of old socks and host a puppet show.** 

6 © IXL Learning

DAY 1 Place value

Color the digit in the given place.

tens place	ones place
82	56
ones place	hundreds place
203	802
hundreds place	tens place
167	941

Read each clue and write the number.

I have exactly 7 tens and 4 ones. What number am I? _____

I have exactly 4 hundreds, 2 tens, and 3 ones. What number am I? _____

I have exactly 1 ten, 8 ones, and 3 hundreds. What number am I? _____

I have exactly 0 ones, 8 hundreds, and 9 tens. What number am I? _____

DAY 1: Synonyms

Match each word to its synonym.

small — tiny

hop   present

gift   noise

sound   house

unhappy   jump

beautiful   pretty

home   steps

grin   finish

end   sad

stairs   smile

DAY 2 — Add and subtract within 20

IXL.com skill ID: **QQP**

Add or subtract.

12 + 3 = _____   9 + 9 = _____   2 + 11 = _____

11 − 5 = _____   13 + 3 = _____   13 − 5 = _____

6 + 8 = _____   17 − 9 = _____   19 − 9 = _____

15 + 4 = _____   14 − 10 = _____   12 + 5 = _____

7 + 13 = _____   19 − 3 = _____   20 − 8 = _____

Write each missing number.

8 + _____ = 12   _____ + 7 = 13   8 + _____ = 16

6 − _____ = 0   _____ + 6 = 16   13 − _____ = 4

_____ − 6 = 11   3 + _____ = 15   _____ − 10 = 8

_____ − 3 = 7   14 − _____ = 7   15 − _____ = 9

12 + _____ = 12   _____ + 11 = 19   20 − _____ = 10

Brain Break! Stand up and stretch your arms above your head. Reach as high as you can!

DAY 2 Reading comprehension

Read the story. Then answer the questions.

Digging In

In April, Thomas and Jake planted lots of tiny seeds in the garden. Day after day, the boys watched the plants grow. After three months, the first vegetables were ready!

"Let's start with the carrots," Thomas said. He took hold of the long green leaves and tugged. He pulled and pulled until the first bright orange carrot suddenly popped up. Thomas handed each carrot he pulled to Jake, who put them in a pile.

After pulling up all the carrots, the boys carried them into the house. They washed off the dirt and put the carrots in a bowl. They were finally ready to taste the carrots that they had planted months ago!

"Time to dig in!" Jake said with a smile.

Who are the characters in the story? _____

What are the characters doing in the story? Put an X next to the correct answer.

_____ planting seeds   _____ gathering carrots   _____ eating carrots

In the picture, which character is on the left? How can you tell? _____

_____

_____

How do the characters feel about their garden? How can you tell? _____

_____

_____

DAY 3: States of matter

Circle to tell whether each item is a solid, a liquid, or a gas.

surfboard	wind	water in a fishbowl
(solid) liquid gas	solid liquid gas	solid liquid gas
air inside of a pool float	**rain**	**towel**
solid liquid gas	solid liquid gas	solid liquid gas
an ocean wave	**sunglasses**	**bubbles in a soda bottle**
solid liquid gas	solid liquid gas	solid liquid gas

DAY 3 Cause and effect

IXL.com skill ID **J68**

Read each pair of sentences. Write a C next to the cause. Write an E next to the effect.

C Jenny stepped in a big puddle.

E Her socks and shoes were wet.

____ Everyone stood up and clapped.

____ The play was over.

____ I washed my hands.

____ My hands were green and sticky.

____ Zuri could not find the light switch.

____ Zuri tripped over a toy on the floor.

____ Mr. Martin rode his bike to work.

____ Mr. Martin could not find his car keys.

____ Juan left his bedroom window open.

____ The wind blew papers off Juan's desk.

Your turn! Think about a cause and effect from your day so far. Write them below.

Cause	
Effect	

DAY 4: Word problems

Answer each question.

In a game of beach volleyball, Imani scores 9 points and Liam scores 5 points. How many points do they score in all?

_____ points

Owen has 12 ice pops in his cooler. He shares 5 of them with his friends. How many ice pops does Owen have left?

_____ ice pops

The Wave Rider is Li's favorite water slide. She rides it 7 times in the morning and 6 times in the afternoon. How many times does Li ride the Wave Rider?

_____ times

Alex won $20 in a sandcastle-building contest. He spends $8 on a new beach towel. How much prize money does he have left over?

_____

Evelyn and Micha paint rocks for their gardens. Evelyn paints 8 rocks. Micha paints 9 rocks. How many rocks do Evelyn and Micha paint in all?

_____ rocks

Henry and Adam draw chalk pictures in their driveway. They draw 14 pictures in all. Henry draws 8 of the pictures. How many pictures does Adam draw?

_____ pictures

DAY 4: Short and long vowel sounds

IXL.com skill ID
C8M

Read each word. Do you hear a short vowel sound or a long vowel sound? Color the raindrops using the key.

BLUE — short vowel sound

ORANGE — long vowel sound

- band
- kind
- flash
- rain
- think
- left
- drum
- night
- kite
- home
- block
- dream
- grin
- moon

LANGUAGE ARTS

DAY 5: Sudoku

Complete the sudoku puzzles using the numbers 1–4. Each number must appear only once in each row, column, and block.

Puzzle 1:
2	1	4	3
	3	2	1
			4
1		3	2

Puzzle 2:
		1	2
	1		3
	2		
4		2	1

Puzzle 3:
	3	2	4
	2		
3			2
2		1	

Puzzle 4:
4			3
		3	4
3	2		4
			2

ENRICHMENT

DAY 5 Word scramble

Unscramble each word! Then fill in the circled letters to reveal the mystery word.

asil

ⓢ a i l

avwe

_ _ ⓪ _

sdna

_ ⓪ _ _

ahskr

⓪ _ _ _ _

rahci

_ ⓪ _ _ _

olceor

_ _ _ _ ⓪ _

twloe

_ _ _ ⓪ _

lgirl

_ ⓪ _ _ _

asdlan

_ _ ⓪ _ _ _ _

Mystery word: Ⓢ ⓪ ⓪ ⓪ ⓪ ⓪ ⓪ ⓪

DAY 6 Consonant blends

IXL.com skill ID
CAV

Write the missing letters.

g i _ _

n e _ _

_ _ i b

d e _ _

_ _ o c k

_ _ i l l

_ _ i n g

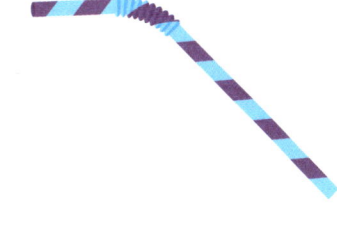

_ _ a w

_ _ a s h

_ _ u _

_ _ a _ _

DAY 6 — Add and subtract

IXL.com skill ID **L7Z**

Add or subtract.

```
  26          43            29
- 15        + 52          + 35
```

```
  25          42            30
+ 62        - 24          + 49
```

```
  78          17            61
- 73        + 63          - 39
```

Follow the path from start to finish.

START → 83

83 — −67 ↓

□ — +82 → □

□ ↑ −39

□ — −24 → □

□ ↓ +45

□ — −53 → □ ↑ +38 — FINISH 65

DAY 7 Reading comprehension

Read the passage and answer the questions. Put an X next to the correct answer, or write your answer on the line.

Forest Flyers

Flying squirrels look a lot like the tree squirrels you might see in parks and backyards. But unlike tree squirrels, they can fly! Well, kind of. Flying squirrels should really be called "gliding squirrels," because they don't really fly at all. They jump through the air to **glide** between trees.

Flying squirrels can travel about 150 feet in one jump. That's half a football field!

Most flying animals use their wings to fly through the air. But the flying squirrel doesn't have wings. Instead, it has a special piece of skin that helps it stay up in the air. This piece of skin stretches between the squirrel's front and back legs. The skin catches the air to help the squirrel glide from tree to tree. The squirrel uses its long, flat tail to turn and slow down before landing.

What is the passage about?

_____ flying squirrels _____ flying animals _____ gray squirrels

What information can you learn from the passage?

_____ Tree squirrels eat nuts and seeds from the forest floor.

_____ Gray squirrels sleep during the day and look for food at night.

_____ Flying squirrels have special body parts to help them get around.

Which word means the same as **glide** as it is used in the passage?

_____ hang _____ soar _____ run _____ climb

What is the main difference between flying squirrels and most flying animals?

_____

DAY 7
Urban, suburban, and rural

IXL.com skill ID
T73

Read the definitions. Then label each community as urban, suburban, or rural.

- An **urban** area is a city. It has many people and buildings.
- A **suburban** area is near a city. It is less crowded than a city. People usually live in houses with yards.
- A **rural** area is much less crowded. Houses are much more spread out. People in rural areas often live on farms or ranches.

_____

_____

_____

_____

_____

_____

Think about where you live. Is it urban, suburban, or rural? How can you tell?

The place where I live is _____. I can tell because _____

_____

_____

_____

SOCIAL STUDIES

DAY 8 — Word problems

IXL.com skill ID
7P8

Ana buys seeds to plant a garden. Use the pictures to answer each question.

How many total pea seeds and tomato seeds does Ana have?

_____ seeds

Ana plants some cucumber seeds. If there are 2 cucumber seeds left in the packet, how many cucumber seeds did she plant?

_____ cucumber seeds

Ana plants 29 pea seeds. How many pea seeds does she have left over?

_____ pea seeds

Ana plants 18 tomato seeds in one row and 18 in another row. How many tomato seeds does she have left over?

_____ tomato seeds

How many total tomato, cucumber, and pea seeds did Ana plant?

_____ seeds

MATH

DAY 8: Capitalization

Circle the words with capitalization errors in each sentence.

Did anyone tell Peter that the (Game) is on (monday)?

Taylor went all the way to New york to see her Aunt.

I help in the Garden on tuesday and Thursday.

Are we driving to mount rushmore in our Tiny car?

It's Only june, but Tess knows what she wants to wear on halloween.

My friend maria went on Vacation to Spain last Summer.

if you live in Canada, you know that it snows A lot in january.

My cousin quinn's Birthday Party is on saturday at the zoo.

The Teacher said keenan and i were the best Swimmers in the class.

One of my Best friends grew up Here, but now She lives in japan.

Write a sentence about a special place. Use correct capitalization, and include at least two proper nouns!

_____

_____

Boost your learning and save 20%!
Scan the QR code or visit www.ixl.com/workbook/23s for details.

DAY 9 — Comparing numbers

IXL.com skill ID **XF9**

Circle the greater number in each pair.

89 92	75 57	648 486
560 506	823 871	329 293
114 141	759 751	652 632

Circle the greatest number in each group.

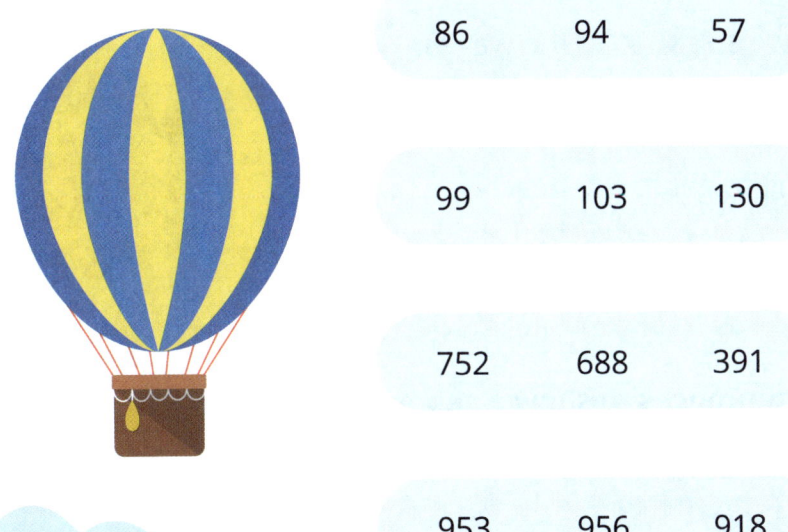

86   94   57

99   103   130

752   688   391

953   956   918

Brain Break!  Stretch out one hand like a starfish. Use the pointer finger on your other hand to trace your fingers slowly. Breathe in as you trace upward. Breathe out as you trace downward.

MATH
23
© IXL Learning

DAY 9: Sequence of events

IXL.com skill ID
5SF

Read the sentences in each group. Look for words that tell you the order of events. Then write a number next to each sentence to put them in order, starting at 1.

_____ After lunch, Ron's puppy played in the mud.

_____ There was a rainstorm this morning.

_____ Before bed, Ron gave his puppy a bath.

_____ After a few hours, the juice pops are ready.

_____ First, we pour juice into paper cups and add sticks.

_____ Then, we put the cups in the freezer.

_____ Today, we are making fruit juice pops.

_____ When we got here, we splashed in the waves.

_____ We will have more time tomorrow to enjoy the beach.

_____ We drove all morning to get to the beach.

_____ Tonight, we will make a campfire on the sand.

Try it yourself! Write your own sentences to show a sequence of events.

1.

2.

3.

4.

DAY 10: Decode the riddles

Solve the riddles. Write each letter of your answer on a line. You can use the secret code below to help you!

What has keys but cannot open locks? $\underline{A}_{8}\ \underline{P}_{1}\ \underline{I}_{4}\ \underline{A}_{8}\ \underline{N}_{12}\ \underline{O}_{3}$

What has hands but cannot clap? $\underline{}_{8}\ \underline{}_{6}\ \underline{}_{7}\ \underline{}_{3}\ \underline{}_{6}\ \underline{}_{14}$

What is full of holes but can still hold water? $\underline{}_{8}\ \underline{}_{10}\ \underline{}_{1}\ \underline{}_{3}\ \underline{}_{12}\ \underline{}_{2}\ \underline{}_{5}$

What comes down but never goes up? $\underline{}_{13}\ \underline{}_{8}\ \underline{}_{4}\ \underline{}_{12}$

What can be broken with just a whisper? $\underline{}_{10}\ \underline{}_{4}\ \underline{}_{7}\ \underline{}_{5}\ \underline{}_{12}\ \underline{}_{6}\ \underline{}_{5}$

What has a neck, no head, and wears a cap? $\underline{}_{8}\ \underline{}_{11}\ \underline{}_{3}\ \underline{}_{15}\ \underline{}_{15}\ \underline{}_{7}\ \underline{}_{5}$

Which word is shorter when you add two letters to it? $\underline{}_{10}\ \underline{}_{20}\ \underline{}_{3}\ \underline{}_{13}\ \underline{}_{15}$

What belongs to you but is used more often by others? $\underline{}_{17}\ \underline{}_{3}\ \underline{}_{19}\ \underline{}_{13}\ \underline{}_{12}\ \underline{}_{8}\ \underline{}_{18}\ \underline{}_{5}$

1	2	3	4	5	6	7	8	9	10	11	12	13	14	15	16	17	18	19	20
P	G	O	I	E	C	L	A	D	S	B	N	R	K	T	F	Y	M	U	H

ENRICHMENT

DAY 10 Logic puzzle

Ming, Tia, Lily, and Brody go to an ice cream stand for frozen treats. Each friend orders a different flavor of ice cream.

Use the clues and the grid to find out which ice cream flavor each friend orders.

- Tia does not order mint ice cream.
- Lily's ice cream is made with sweet red fruit.
- Ming chooses a flavor that is not made from fruit.
- Brody orders an ice cream flavor that starts with the same letter as his name.

	Peach	Blackberry	Strawberry	Mint
Ming				
Tia				
Lily				
Brody				

Use your answers from the grid to finish the sentences.

Ming orders _____ ice cream.

Tia orders _____ ice cream.

Lily orders _____ ice cream.

Brody orders _____ ice cream.

DAY 11 — Three-digit addition

Add.

```
  532        638        270
+ 465      + 127      + 152
```

```
  463        160        583
+  85      + 735      +  97
```

```
  326        357        193
+ 466      + 244      + 205
```

Write each missing digit.

```
  3 4 1      5 9 7      4 1 6
+ 2 3 ▢    + 3 ▢ 7    + 4 2 ▢
  5 7 6      9 0 4      8 4 0
```

```
  1 4 ▢      2 9 ▢      5 ▢ 3
+ ▢ 6 3    + 6 7 4    + 2 2 ▢
  9 1 2    ▢ 7 2        8 0 1
```

DAY 11 Reading comprehension

Read the story. Then answer the questions.

Pilot Parade

"Do you see her?" asked Dottie's big sister, Ruth. The girls were waiting with the crowd along First Street for the parade to begin.

"Not yet," replied Dottie. Last year, in 1928, there was a big parade for Amelia Earhart in New York City. Ruth and Dottie had seen a photo of the parade. The picture showed a huge crowd and even bigger buildings. Dottie didn't like crowds or buildings, but she liked the sky. She dreamed of being a bold, fearless pilot just like Amelia Earhart.

Just then, the crowd roared. Dottie stood on her tiptoes to see, but a man stepped in front of her, waving his arms. She saw a flash of yellow down the street. The car had almost reached them, and she still didn't have a clear view. But Dottie knew that pilots had to be bold. So she ducked under the man's arm, quick as a wink.

"It's her!" exclaimed Dottie. A woman wearing a pilot's jacket waved to the crowd from the front seat of the car. As Dottie lifted her arms and cheered loudly, Amelia turned. Dottie was sure she saw the pilot smiling and waving directly at her.

What is the setting? _____

Who is the main character? _____

What is the problem in the story? _____
_____

What is the solution? _____
_____

DAY 12 Antonyms

IXL.com skill ID **9Y4**

Write an antonym for each word. Then fill in the circled letters to reveal the mystery word. Answer the question that follows.

clean   d i (r) t y

begin   (_) _ _

large   _ (_) _ _ _

asleep   _ _ _ _ (_)

top   _ _ _ _ (_)

ahead   (_) _ _ _ _

real   _ _ _ (_)

late   _ _ (_) _ _

Mystery word: (r)(_)(_)(_)(_)(_)(_)

What is an antonym of the mystery word? _____

Brain Break! Give a big hug to a family member, a pet, or your favorite stuffed animal!

LANGUAGE ARTS

DAY 12: Three-digit subtraction

Subtract.

```
  936        483        809
- 215      - 179      -  93
-----      -----      -----
```

```
  521        775        285
- 370      - 535      - 243
-----      -----      -----
```

```
  453        612        846
- 106      - 449      - 752
-----      -----      -----
```

Write each missing digit.

```
  1 6 5        9 4 ☐        ☐ 2 0
-     3 ☐    - 3 0 8      - 3 9 8
-------      -------      -------
  1 3 2        6 3 6        4 2 2
```

```
  9 3 4        4 0 ☐        7 ☐ 2
- 5 ☐ 7      - ☐ 5 6      - 5 9 ☐
-------      -------      -------
    4 0 ☐      2 4 4        1 0 6
```

DAY 13 — Natural resources

Natural resources are useful things that come directly from nature. They are not made by people.

Look at the picture. Then answer the questions.

List **five** natural resources you see in the picture. _____

_____

Is a playground slide a natural resource? How do you know? _____

_____

_____

Water is an important natural resource. How is water useful to people? _____

_____

_____

DAY 13 Consonant digraphs

When two letters come together to make one sound, they are called a **digraph**. Some consonant digraphs are **ch**, **sh**, **th**, **ph**, and **wh**.

Write the missing letters.

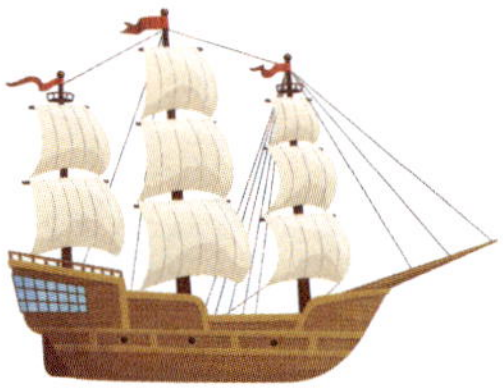

__ i p	b a __ __	f i __ __
t r a __ __	g r a __ __	__ __ u m b
__ __ e e l	c o u __ __	E a r __ __
__ __ i c k	__ __ o t o	p e a __ __

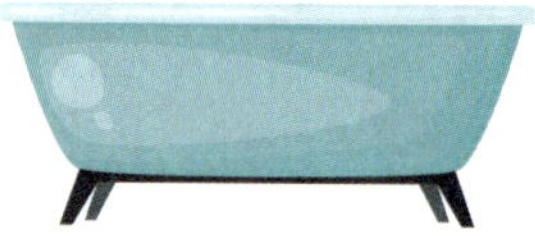

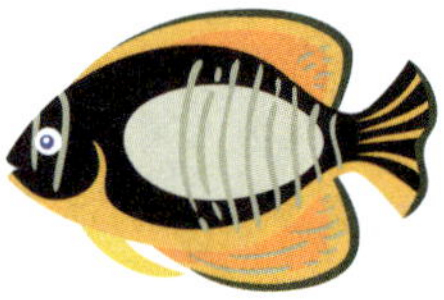

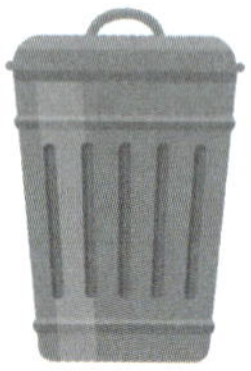

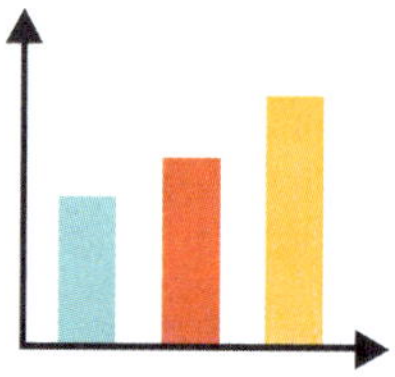

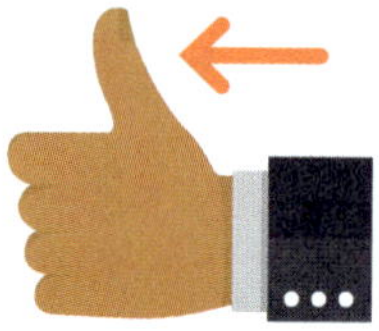

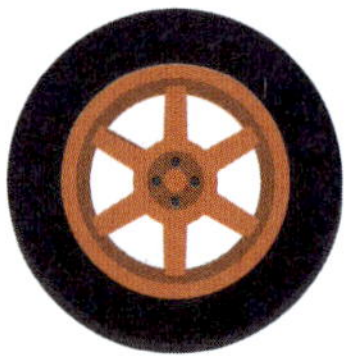

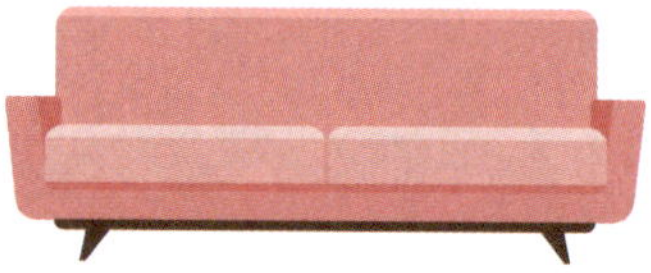

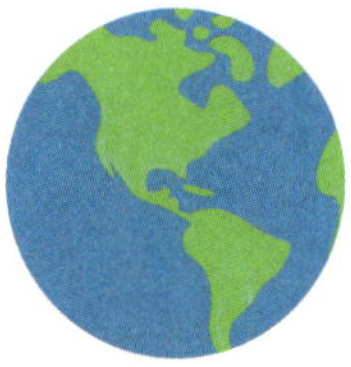

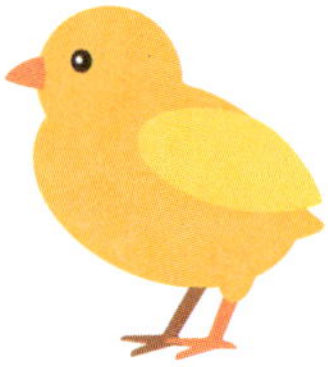

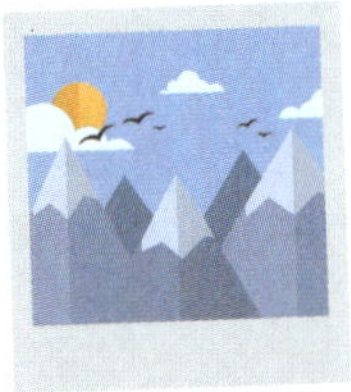

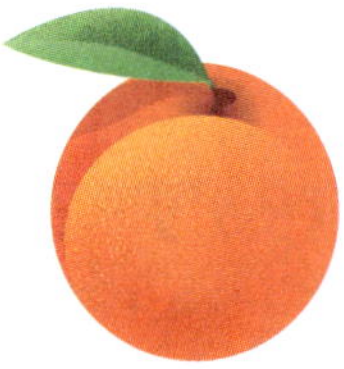

DAY 14 Telling time

Write the time shown on each clock.

_____ _____ _____

_____ _____ _____

Draw hands on each clock to show the time.

DAY 14 Fact or opinion

IXL.com skill ID **79N**

A **fact** is something that can be proved right or wrong. An **opinion** is something that a person believes, thinks, or feels. An opinion cannot be proved right or wrong.

Read each sentence. Write an F next to each fact. Write an O next to each opinion.

O	Green apples taste better than red ones.	____	My dad sometimes puts an orange in my lunch.
____	My sister will not eat apples.	____	Popcorn with butter is the best snack there is.
____	Hot dogs should always come with chili.	____	I have eggs every morning for breakfast.
____	Cheese pizza isn't as good as pepperoni pizza.	____	Ice cream is too cold to eat in the winter.
____	Eva drinks milk three times a day.	____	Mixed berries are a nice treat.
____	Cakes can be made with flour, sugar, and butter.	____	Max likes lemon pancakes.

Your turn! Write one fact and one opinion about food in the spaces below.

Fact	
Opinion	

34 © IXL Learning   LANGUAGE ARTS

DAY 15 — Word categories

IXL.com skill ID **KGD**

Sort the words into categories to solve the puzzle. Each category will contain three words. Each word will be used in only one category.

~~leaf~~	toss	basket	trunk
box	meow	chest	cook
crack	bark	oink	moo

Category	Word 1	Word 2	Word 3
Parts of a tree	leaf		
Animal sounds			
Places where items are kept			
Things you can do with an egg			

Get ahead of the curve with extra practice!
Join IXL today. Scan the QR code or visit www.ixl.com/workbook/23s for details.

DAY 15 Scavenger hunt

It's time for a scavenger hunt! Find a different item for each clue. Write the name of each item you find next to the clue.

Something with wheels	
Something made of metal	
Something that is wet	
Something that is noisy	
Something that is colorful	
Something that is tiny	
Something that feels smooth	
Something that feels rough	
Something that blows in the wind	
Something that grows from a seed	
Something that is shaped like a sphere	

Weeks 4–6: Overview

Week 4

Math
Addition and subtraction word problems
Repeated addition

Language arts
Vowel teams
Author's purpose
Opinion writing

Social studies
Producers and consumers

Enrichment
Design a water bottle

Week 5

Math
Modeling multiplication
Naming equal parts

Language arts
Complete sentences
R-controlled vowels
Prefixes

Science
Temperature

Enrichment
Imaginary vehicles
Connect the shapes

Week 6

Math
Making equal parts
Multiplication word problems

Language arts
Compare and contrast
Vowel sounds in closed syllables
Strong verbs

Social studies
Landmarks and monuments

Enrichment
Fill-in-the-blank story

More ways to learn

Keep the learning going! Use these simple, exciting activities to help you stay active, curious, and creative during your summer break.

See how many activities you can do! Cross off each activity as you complete it.

Watch a sunrise or a sunset.	Make a boat that floats.	Paint fun designs on smooth rocks.
Choose a place on a map or globe and research five facts about it.	Help a family member or neighbor with something.	Make ice pops using fruit juice.
Soak a sponge in water and use it to play catch outside with a friend.	Go camping, indoors or outdoors.	Make a paper chain using construction paper.

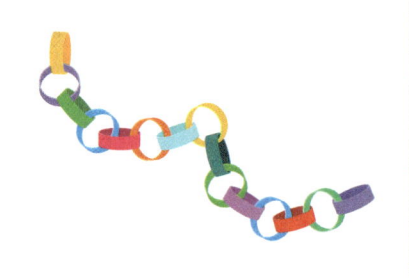

DAY 16: Vowel teams

Sometimes two vowels work together as a **vowel team**. The first vowel in a vowel team says its name. It makes a long vowel sound. The second vowel is silent.

Complete each word with the correct vowel team. Some vowel teams will be used more than once.

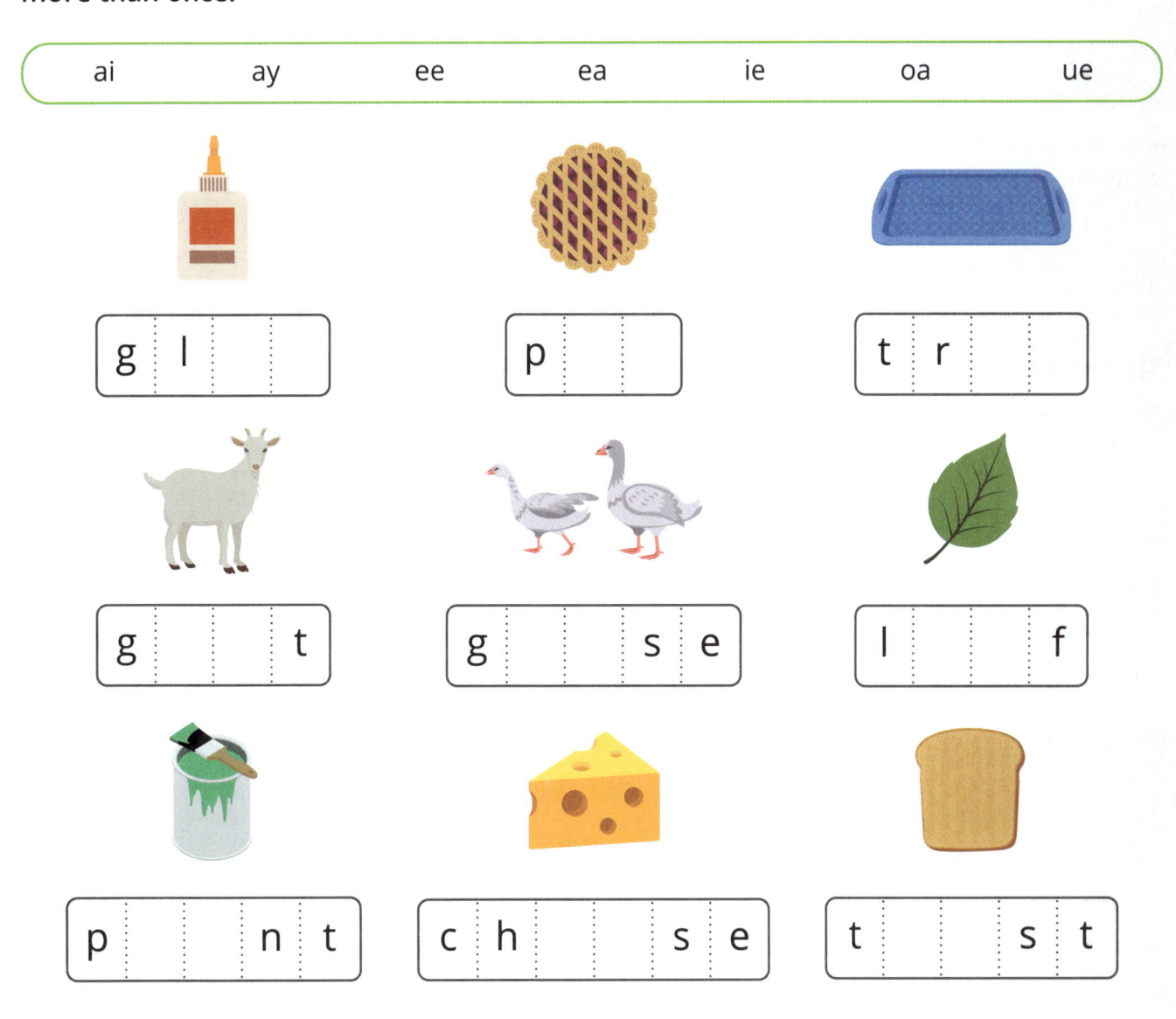

> ai   ay   ee   ea   ie   oa   ue

g l _ _ _

p _ _

t r _ _

g _ _ t

g _ _ s e

l _ _ f

p _ _ n t

c h _ _ s e

t _ _ s t

Say each word out loud. What long vowel sound do you hear? Color the words above using the key.

- **RED** — long a sound
- **GREEN** — long e sound
- **PURPLE** — long i sound
- **YELLOW** — long o sound
- **BLUE** — long u sound

DAY 16: Word problems

Pine Grove Summer Camp is open to campers! Answer each question.

There are 654 campers and 82 staff members at the camp. How many people are there in all?

_____ people

At the ropes course, 358 campers climb on the low ropes, and 216 campers climb on the high ropes. How many more campers climb on the low ropes than on the high ropes?

_____ more campers

The staff buys 900 marshmallows for s'mores night. The staff and campers eat 832 marshmallows. How many marshmallows are left over?

_____ marshmallows

The talent show is coming up. In all, 350 campers try out. Of those campers, 108 sing and 45 dance for their acts. How many of the campers who try out for the show do not sing or dance for their acts?

_____ campers

The campers are sailing model boats on the lake. They start with 276 boats, but 184 of those boats sink. Then they recover 93 of the boats that sank. How many boats do they have now?

_____ boats

DAY 17: Complete sentences

A **sentence** is a group of words that forms a complete thought.

- A **complete sentence** has both a subject and a verb.
- A **sentence fragment** is a group of words that does not express a complete thought. It is usually missing a subject or a verb.
- A **run-on sentence** is made up of two sentences that should each stand alone.

Color the boxes using the key.

YELLOW — complete sentence

BLUE — sentence fragment

RED — run-on sentence

We listened to the singer's newest song.	Michael's bright blue glasses.	Strawberries are not berries bananas are.	Most octopuses like to live alone.
Cold water on a hot afternoon.	My dog has a pile of sticks from our walks.	Forgot to bring my towel.	I love going to the lake we swim all day.
A giraffe has a long neck it can reach the leaves in tall trees.	After I found the perfect headphones for my birthday.	I baked fresh chocolate chip cookies with my sister.	The boys made a smoothie it was delicious.

DAY 17: Producers and consumers

IXL.com skill ID **FBZ**

Every good or service has a producer and a consumer. A **producer** makes a good or provides a service. A **consumer** buys a good or service.

Read each story. Who is the producer? Who is the consumer? Write their names.

Story	Producer	Consumer
Jackson is a baker. He makes cupcakes. Kristen buys cupcakes from Jackson.	Jackson	Kristen
Stella is a farmer. She grows apples. Eric buys apples from Stella.		
Jason buys a painting from Luna at her studio. Luna is a painter.		
Eliza is a cook. Carlos orders lunch from her every Friday.		
Cory buys a book written by her favorite author, Noah.		
Ethan makes lemonade. Carmen buys lemonade from Ethan at his lemonade stand.		
Seth pays Ashley to fix his bike. Ashley owns a bike repair shop.		
Ryan is a gardener. Kayla pays Ryan to take care of her plants.		

Try it yourself! Write your own story with a producer and a consumer.

Story	Producer	Consumer

DAY 18: Repeated addition

IXL.com skill ID **PNR**

Write a repeated addition equation to find each total.

_____ + _____ = _____ tulips

_____ + _____ + _____ = _____ towels

_____ + _____ + _____ = _____ flip flops

_____ + _____ = _____ chocolates

_____ tennis balls

_____ bananas

Brain Break! Close your eyes, take a deep breath, and focus on each part of your body. Start at the top of your head and go all the way down to your toes. Then go all the way back up again.

Reading comprehension

Read the flyer and answer the questions. Put an X next to the correct answer, or write your answer on the line.

BAKE SALE
TO SUPPORT THE
Arlington Community Swim Team

Get your sweet tooth ready and help raise money for the team to travel to swim meets this summer! All treats will be made by Mr. and Mrs. Fletcher of Fletcher's Bakery, so you know the baked goods are sure to be delicious.

WHEN: Saturday, June 14
12:00–3:00 p.m.

WHERE: Arlington Community Pool

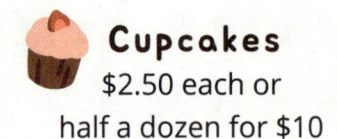

Cookies
$1 each or
6 for $5

Brownies
$2 each or
3 for $5

Cupcakes
$2.50 each or
half a dozen for $10

What is the purpose of the flyer?

_____ to persuade people to come to a bake sale

_____ to inform people about how to host a bake sale

_____ to entertain people with a story about a bake sale

Why is the community having a bake sale?

_____ to raise money to repair the Arlington Community Pool

_____ to raise money for the Arlington Community Swim Team to travel

_____ to raise money for Mr. and Mrs. Fletcher of Fletcher's Bakery

Where will the bake sale be held? _____

Who is making the baked goods for the bake sale? _____

DAY 19: Opinion writing

Read the definitions and sentences. Then label each sentence in the groups below. Use O for opinion, R for reason, and E for example.

An **opinion** shows what the writer believes, thinks, or feels.	A **reason** supports the opinion. It tells why the writer has that opinion.	An **example** supports the reason.
I believe goldfish make better pets than dogs.	It takes less time to take care of a goldfish than to take care of a dog.	For example, goldfish do not need to go on long walks every day.

____ For example, last week, we read a book about honeybees.

____ I love visiting the library with my grandma.

____ We find a new topic to learn about each week.

____ I think that we should move the flower pots into the shade.

____ You can see that the white flowers are turning brown.

____ The flowers are getting too much sun.

____ There are a lot of activities you can do at the Grand Canyon.

____ Hiking is one activity you can do at the Grand Canyon.

____ The Grand Canyon seems like a fun place to visit.

Now you try! Write an example that supports the opinion and reason.

Opinion: Summer is the best season.

Reason: The warm weather is perfect for outdoor adventures.

Example: _____

DAY 19
Repeated addition

IXL.com skill ID
W8T

Write a repeated addition equation to find the total number of dots in each picture. Add the rows.

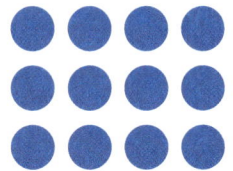

____ + ____ = ____

____ + ____ + ____ + ____ = ____

____ + ____ + ____ = ____

____ + ____ = ____

_____   _____

MATH

DAY 20: Design a water bottle

Design a water bottle to sell! What will make people want to buy it? Use colored pencils or crayons to show your design below. You can add colors, words, and images to your design. On the next page, answer questions about your water bottle.

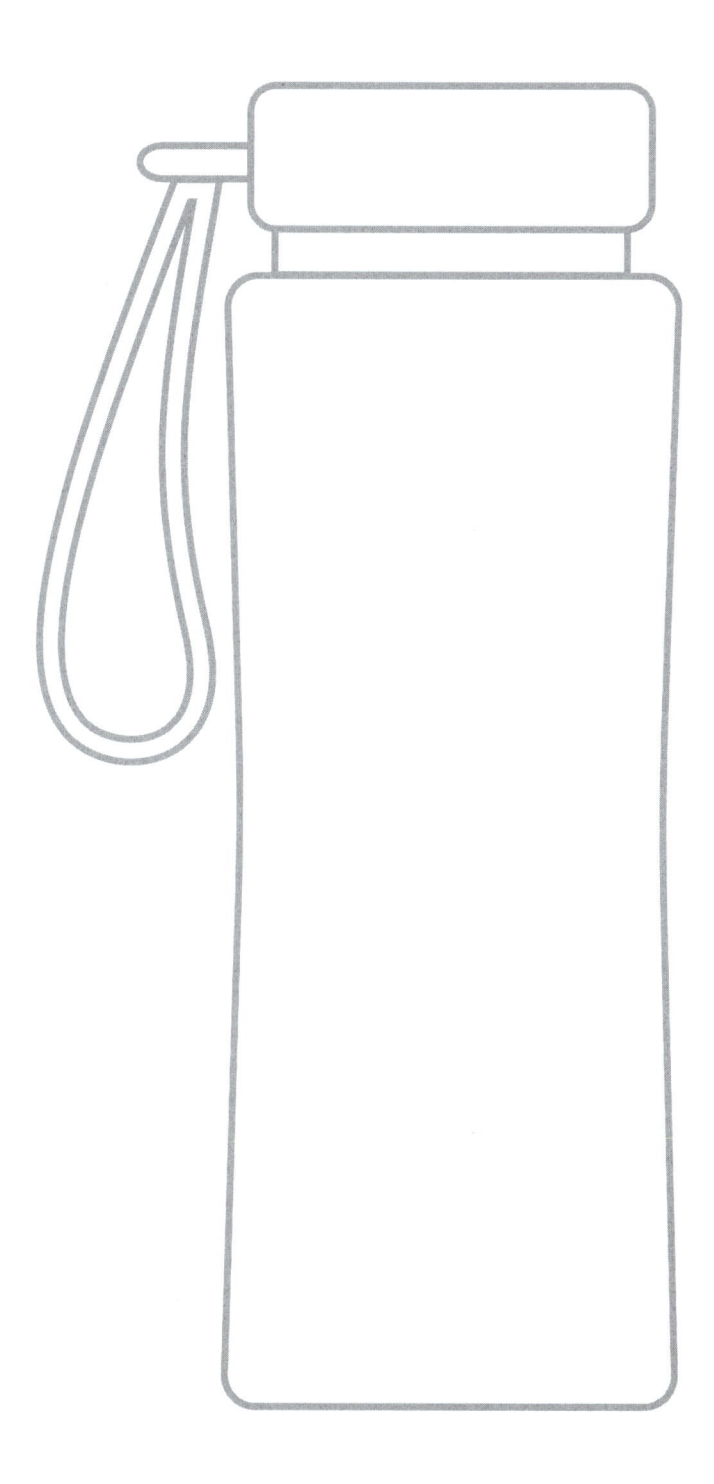

ENRICHMENT

47

DAY 20: Design a water bottle

IXL.com skill ID **5UN**

Tell all about your water bottle! Answer each question.

Describe your water bottle. _____

_____

_____

Why should someone buy your water bottle? Give **three** reasons. Write your reasons in a paragraph.

_____

_____

_____

_____

_____

_____

How much will your water bottle cost (to the nearest dollar)? _____

Imagine you sell 5 water bottles. How much money would you make? Show your work using the number line. _____

⟵—————————————————————————⟶

ENRICHMENT

DAY 21 Repeated addition

IXL.com skill ID **9H2**

Write a repeated addition equation to answer each question. Then show the repeated addition as equal groups.

How many slices of bread are there?

__2 + 2 + 2 = 6__ slices of bread

__3__ groups of __2__ = __6__

How many eggs are there?

_____ eggs

_____ groups of _____ = _____

How many petals are there?

_____ petals

_____ groups of _____ = _____

How many scoops of ice cream are there?

_____ scoops of ice cream

_____ groups of _____ = _____

DAY 21: Sentence scramble

The words in each sentence below are all mixed up! Rearrange the words to make a sentence. Be sure to use correct capitalization and punctuation.

sick Logan today is

Logan is sick today.

is hard raining it

sister run home a my hit

play to you outside do want

I swimming by whales saw the boat

winter the some south fly birds for

library should return Ben to that the book

Reading comprehension

Read the story. Then answer the questions.

Hermit Crab's Perfect Shell

Hermit Crab lived on a sandy beach. All his friends had shells in fancy shapes and bright colors. But Hermit Crab's shell was simple and plain, like the sand. So when his boring shell began to feel too small, he knew it was his chance to find the perfect shell.

First, he found a long shell with brown stripes. He tried it on, but it was too heavy. The next shell he found was even more exciting! It was shiny and green. But it was too big.

Next, Hermit Crab walked past a shell that seemed to be the right size. But it was plain, just like his old shell. No thanks! Instead, he tried one with lots of interesting bumps, but he could barely get one leg in.

Hermit Crab frowned. Suddenly, he saw a shadow flying above him and heard a hungry seagull's loud cry. With no shell and nowhere to hide, he had to act fast. Hermit Crab looked back at the plain shell he had passed. He hurried inside it, safe from the greedy bird. To Hermit Crab's surprise, the plain shell fit just right.

He peeked out from the shell. The seagull was gone, and he was safe. Snuggling back inside the shell, Hermit Crab smiled. He had found his perfect shell after all.

Why did Hermit Crab think the last shell was perfect after all? _____

_____

_____

What is the lesson of this story? Put an X next to the correct answer.

____ It's important to have fancy things.

____ What you want isn't always what you need.

____ You should always follow your dreams.

DAY 22: Understanding temperature

IXL.com skill ID **FYA**

Temperature tells you how hot or cold something is. A **thermometer** is a tool that measures temperature in degrees Celsius (°C) or degrees Fahrenheit (°F).

Write the temperature shown by each thermometer. Write the symbol for degrees (°) and either C for Celsius or F for Fahrenheit.

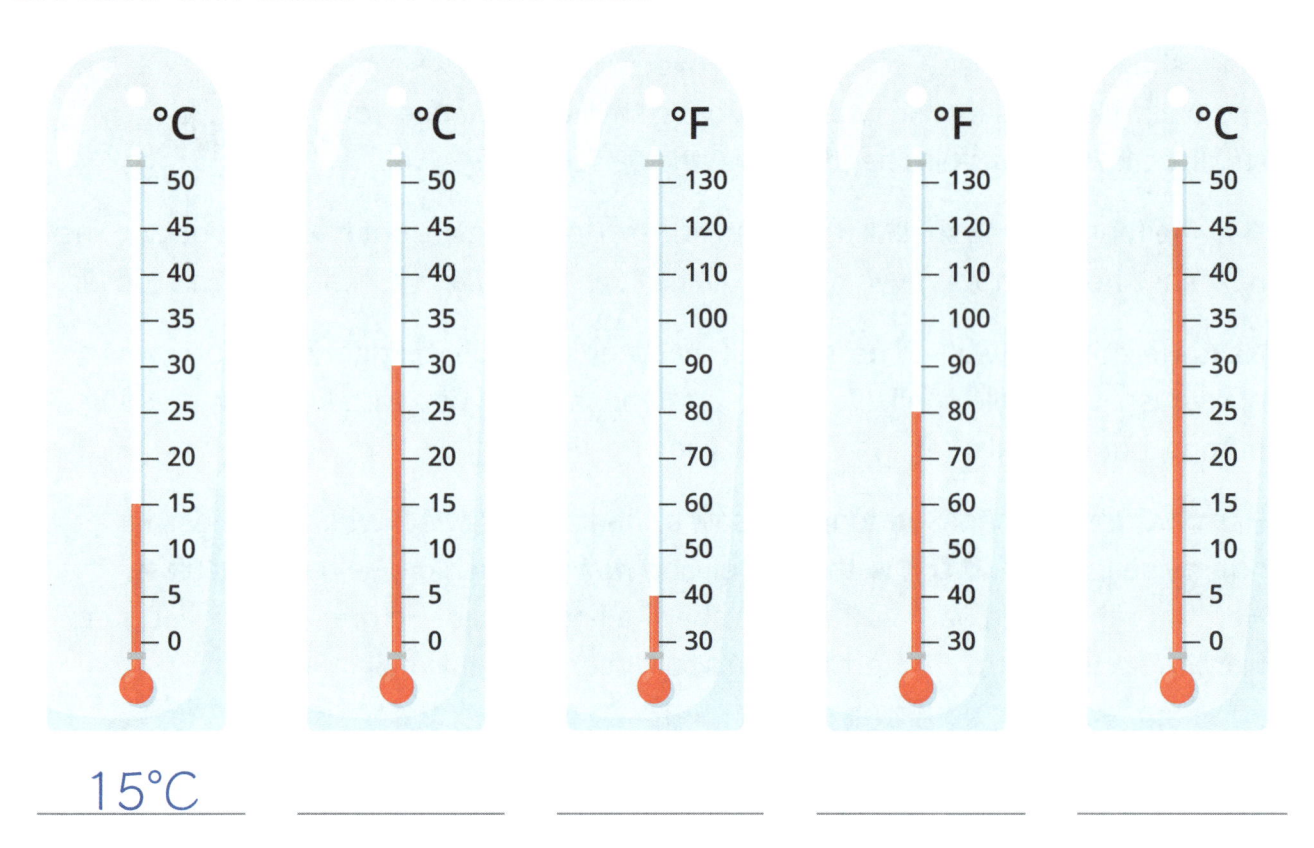

15°C   _____   _____   _____   _____

Answer each question.

It was 5°C when Mia woke up. It was 15°C warmer at lunchtime. What was the temperature at lunchtime?   _____

It was 75°F when Caleb went to the park. It was 10°F cooler when he left. What was the temperature when Caleb left the park?   _____

It was 60°F on Monday afternoon. It was 25°F cooler on Tuesday morning. What was the temperature on Tuesday morning?   _____

DAY 23: Modeling multiplication

You can show equal groups as multiplication. Write the missing numbers to answer each question. Follow the example.

How many wheels are there?

__4__ groups of __2__ = __8__

__4__ × __2__ = __8__ wheels

How many cupcakes are there?

_____ groups of _____ = _____

_____ × _____ = _____ cupcakes

How many slices of lemon are there?

_____ groups of _____ = _____

_____ × _____ = _____ slices of lemon

How many leaves are there?

_____ groups of _____ = _____

_____ × _____ = _____ leaves

DAY 23: R-controlled vowels

When a vowel is followed by the letter **r**, the **r** sometimes changes the sound of the vowel. Some **r-controlled vowel patterns** are **ar**, **er**, **ir**, **or**, and **ur**.

Write the missing letters.

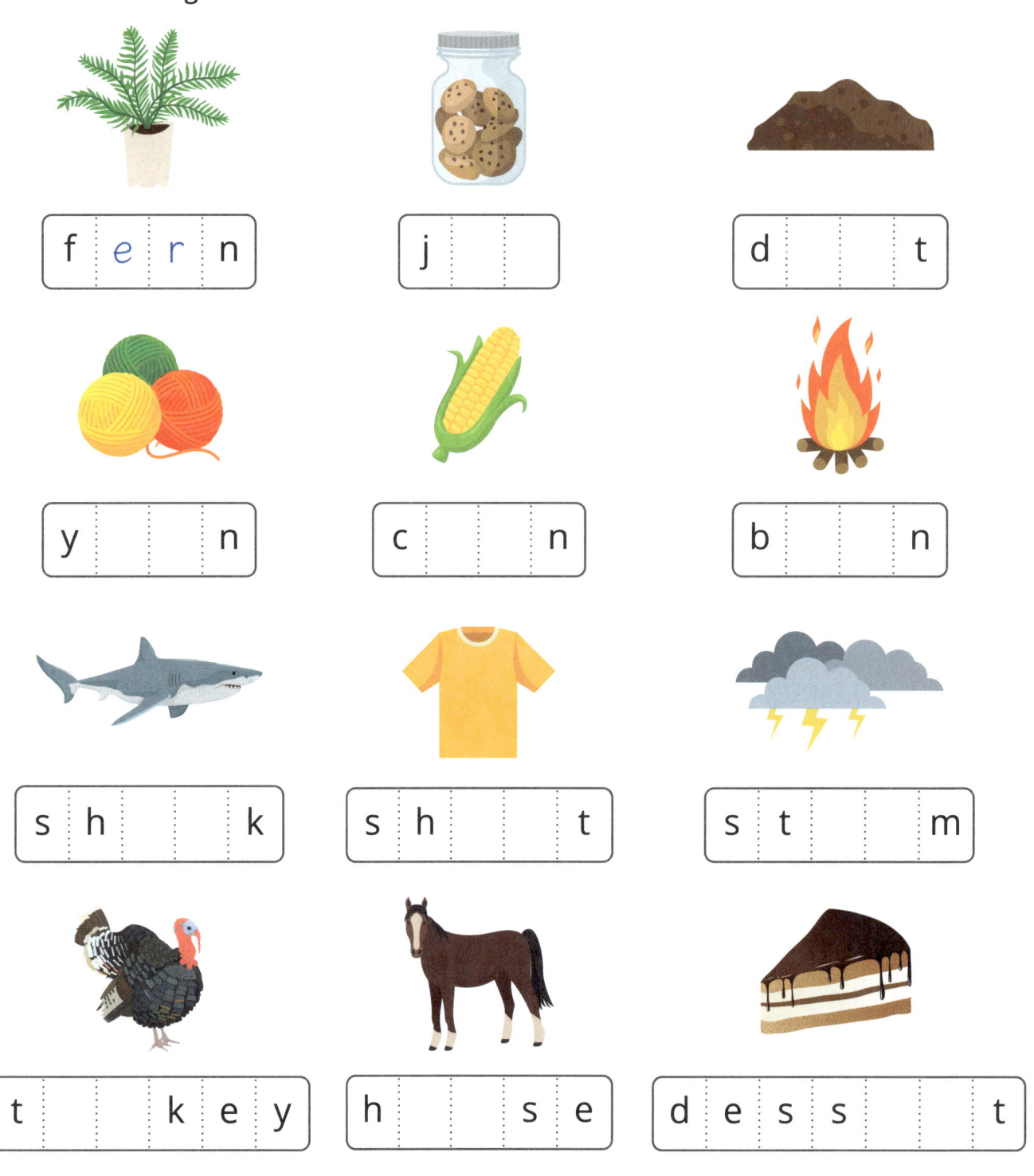

f [e] [r] n

j [ ] [ ] [ ]

d [ ] [ ] t

y [ ] [ ] n

c [ ] [ ] n

b [ ] [ ] n

s h [ ] [ ] k

s h [ ] [ ] t

s t [ ] [ ] m

t [ ] [ ] k e y

h [ ] [ ] s e

d e s s [ ] [ ] t

DAY 24 — Prefixes

IXL.com skill ID **KQY**

A **prefix** can be added to the beginning of a word. It changes the meaning of the word.

Prefix	Meaning	Example
pre-	before	**Pre**wash means *to wash before*.
re-	again	**Re**visit means *to visit again*.
mis-	incorrectly	**Mis**count means *to count incorrectly*.

Circle the correct meaning of each word.

mismatch	match again	match incorrectly
reuse	use again	use before
preheat	heat before	heat again
recharge	charge incorrectly	charge again
mishear	hear incorrectly	hear before
prepay	pay again	pay before
reenter	enter incorrectly	enter again
misspell	spell before	spell incorrectly
precheck	check before	check incorrectly
rebuild	build again	build before

Brain Break! Balance a pillow on your head. How fast can you walk? How far can you go? Can you sit down and get back up again?

LANGUAGE ARTS

DAY 24 Equal parts

Each shape below has been split into equal parts. Write the name for the parts in each shape. You can write halves, thirds, fourths, sixths, or eighths.

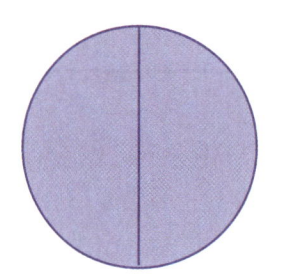

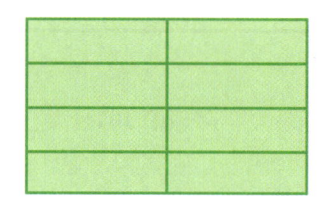

_____sixths_____   _____   _____

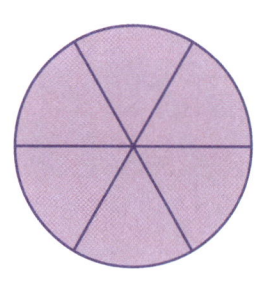

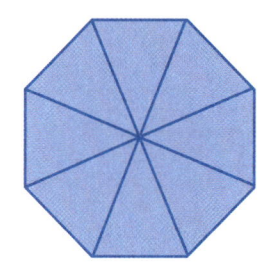

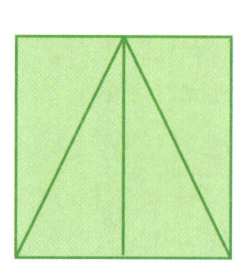

_____   _____   _____

_____   _____   _____

DAY 25: Imaginary vehicles

Time to get creative! Draw new vehicles based on the prompts.

A car with spider legs	A boat with robot arms
A bike that can swim	**A bus that can fly**

ENRICHMENT

Day 25: Connect the shapes

Draw lines to connect the shapes that match. Be sure to follow these rules:

- Your lines must go up, down, left, or right. No diagonal lines are allowed.
- Your lines should not cross any other shapes.
- Your lines should not cross any of your other lines.
- Each puzzle should have all four pairs of shapes connected.

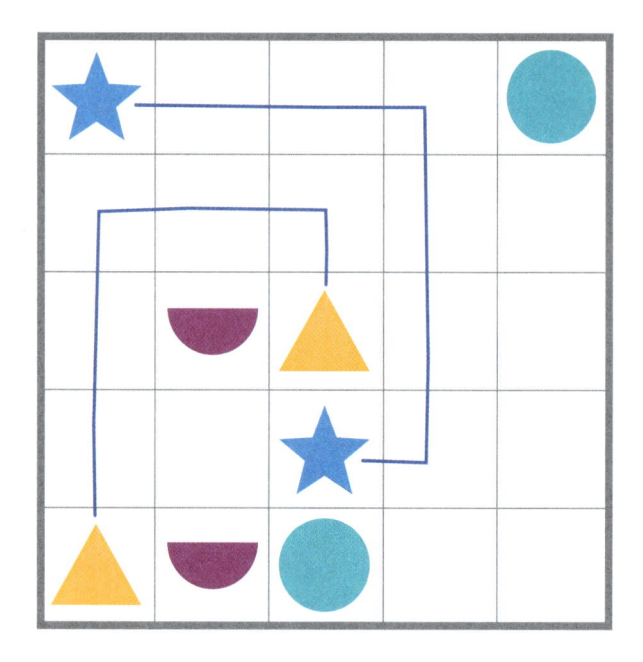

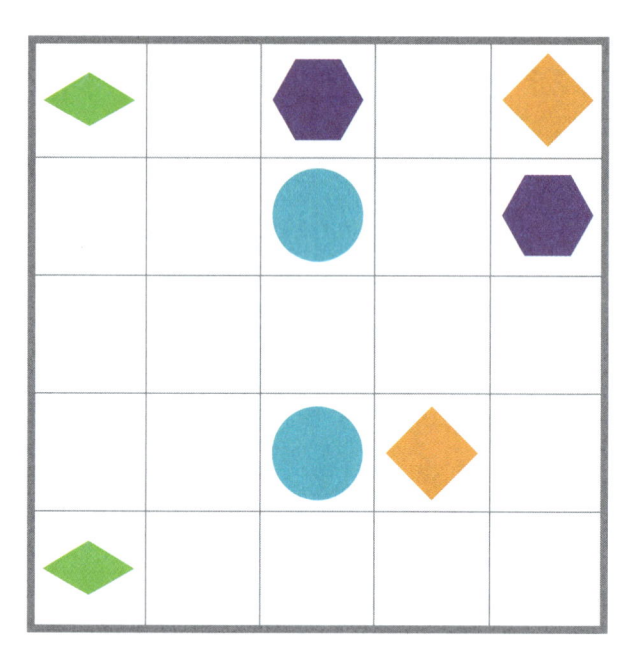

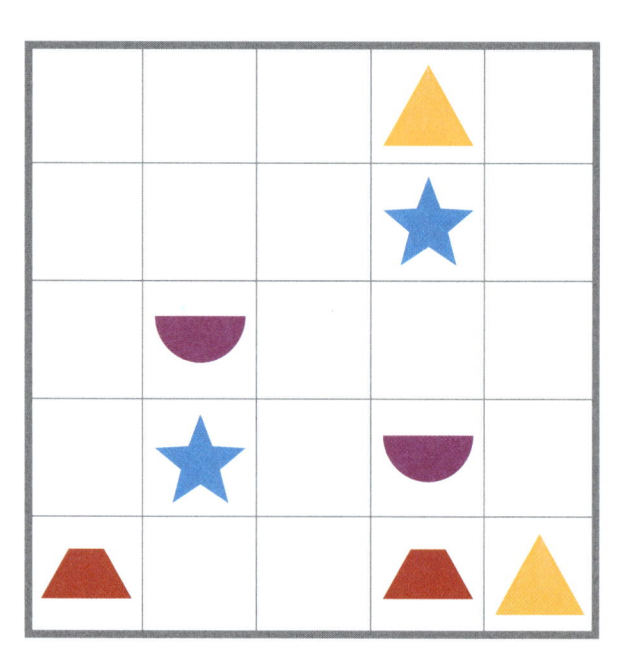

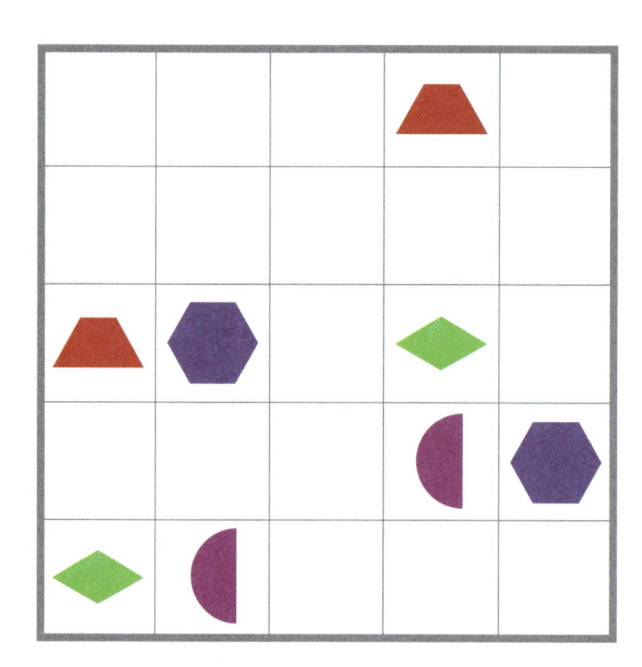

Compare and contrast

Read the passage. Then complete the table with details from the text.

Cheetahs and Leopards

Cheetahs and leopards are wild cats from Africa. Both are known as fast runners and silent hunters. They both have whiskers, long tails, and spots. These big cats have a lot in common, so it can be easy to get them mixed up. But there are some key differences between them.

Even though cheetahs and leopards look alike, their spots can help you tell them apart. A cheetah's spots are round and black, while a leopard's spots are open shapes called rosettes.

Cheetahs are much faster than leopards. While leopards can run about thirty-six miles per hour, cheetahs can run up to seventy-five miles per hour.

Another difference is that cheetahs hunt during the day, and leopards hunt at night. But both of these animals are top hunters in the places where they live.

Include **two** facts in each section of the table.

Both cheetahs and leopards	
• •	
Cheetahs	Leopards
• •	• •

Modeling multiplication

Write an equation to match each model.

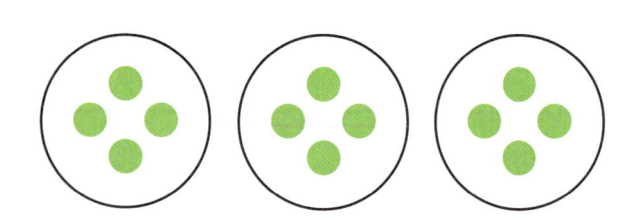

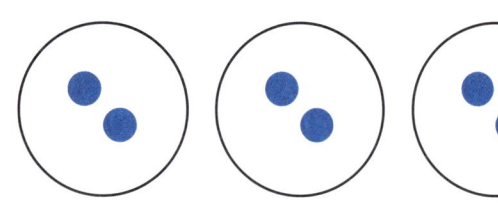

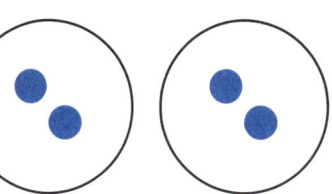

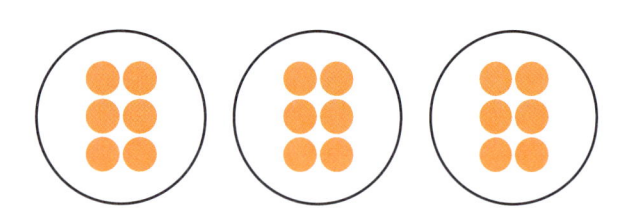

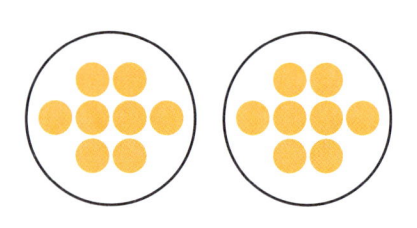

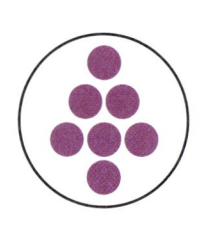

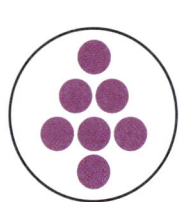

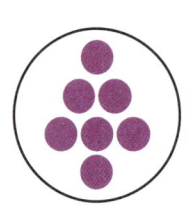

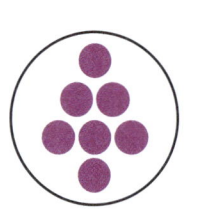

3 × 4 = 12

___ × ___ = ___

___ × ___ = ___

___ × ___ = ___

___ × ___ = ___

DAY 27: Vowel sounds in closed syllables

IXL.com skill ID **XMQ**

A **closed syllable** has one vowel and ends in a consonant.

- A closed syllable usually makes a **short vowel sound**, like in the word **trip**.
- Some closed syllables make a **long vowel sound**, like in the word **old**.

Color the clouds using the key. Notice which words make a long vowel sound instead of a short vowel sound.

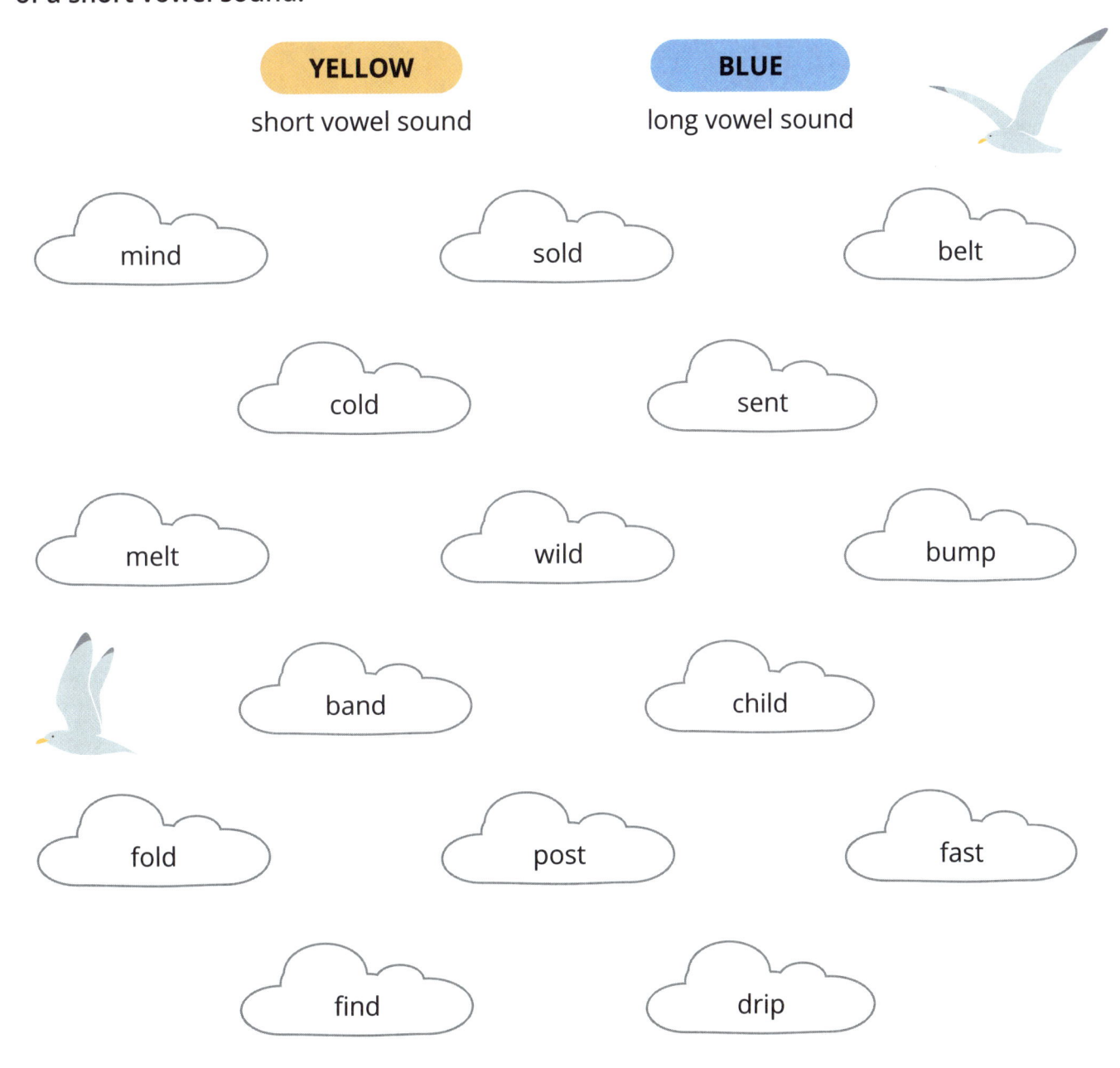

YELLOW — short vowel sound

BLUE — long vowel sound

- mind
- sold
- belt
- cold
- sent
- melt
- wild
- bump
- band
- child
- fold
- post
- fast
- find
- drip

LANGUAGE ARTS

DAY 27 Equal parts

Split each shape into the given parts.

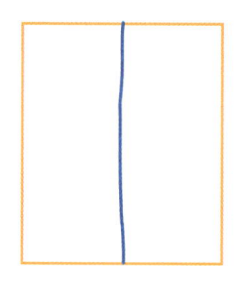

halves

fourths

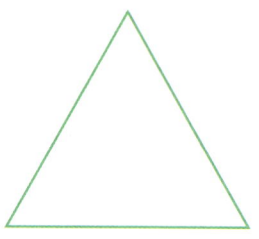

halves

thirds

sixths

eighths

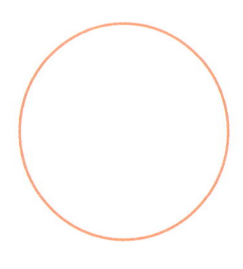

thirds

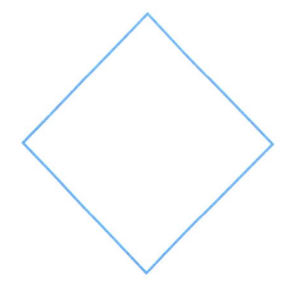

fourths

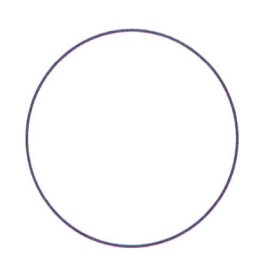

eighths

DAY 28

Landmarks and monuments

IXL.com skill ID
DUU

Use the clues to name each American landmark and monument.

The Statue of Liberty	The Washington Monument	The White House
The Golden Gate Bridge	The Lincoln Memorial	The Gateway Arch

I am a gift from France. I stand in New York Harbor. What am I?

_____

I celebrate a president who led the U.S. during the Civil War. What am I?

_____

I am a long bridge in San Francisco, California. What am I?

_____

I rise high above the Mississippi River in St. Louis, Missouri. What am I?

_____

I celebrate the first president of the U.S. What am I?

_____

I am the home of the president in Washington, D.C. What am I?

_____

Brain Break! Name one thing that starts with each letter of the alphabet. See how fast you can go!

SOCIAL STUDIES

DAY 28 Strong verbs

IXL.com skill ID **LZV**

Strong verbs make your writing more interesting. They give a better picture of what is happening. Circle the stronger verb for each sentence.

Grandma tells | (whispers) a bedtime story to Aidan to help him fall asleep.

Juliette peeked | looked over the fence to see her neighbor's beautiful garden.

Five playful kittens come | bounce into the room and start playing.

My brother begged | asked our parents to let him have a pool party.

The glass cup fell | crashed to the ground and broke into tiny pieces.

After a long day of hiking, Sophia sits | plops down on the couch.

Revise each sentence using a stronger verb. Write the verb on the line.

Hudson ___*drags*___ the heavy box across the floor.
                moves

The cousins quickly _____ out of the pool when the rain started.
                                got

We watch the players _____ across the field.
                                run

The actor _____ angrily across the stage.
                     walked

Early this morning, Miles _____ on the door until we woke up.
                                     knocked

The colorful hot-air balloons _____ through the sky at sunset.
                                         fly

64 © IXL Learning   LANGUAGE ARTS

DAY 29 Word problems

Fill in the blanks to answer each question.

Mr. Harris carries 2 trays. Each tray has 3 glasses of lemonade. How many total glasses of lemonade does Mr. Harris carry?

_____ × _____ = _____

_____ glasses of lemonade

Camila picks 2 pea pods from her garden. Each pea pod has 7 peas in it. How many peas are in the pods in all?

_____ × _____ = _____

_____ peas

Eddie sees 2 sea stars. Each sea star has 5 arms. How many arms do the sea stars have in all?

_____ × _____ = _____

_____ arms

Mira has 2 boxes of colored pencils. Each box has 9 colored pencils. How many total colored pencils does Mira have?

_____ × _____ = _____

_____ colored pencils

DAY 29 Contractions

IXL.com skill ID **WJR**

A **contraction** is a shortened form of two words. An apostrophe (') shows where one or more letters are left out.

Write the contraction.

have not	haven't	I am	
it is		do not	
we are		does not	
did not		you are	
we will		were not	
is not		he will	

Each contraction below is missing an apostrophe. Write the correct contraction. Then write the words that make up the contraction.

arent	aren't	are not
wasnt		
theyre		
shell		
wont		

DAY 30
Fill-in-the-blank story

Complete the chart with words that match the details in the left column. Then use your words to make a silly story on the next page.

Adjective 1	
Plural noun 1	
Plural noun 2	
Feeling	
Adjective 2	
Plural noun 3	
Adjective 3	
Noun	
Color	
Adjective 4	
Adjective 5	
Past-tense verb	
Plural animal	
Food	
Drink	
Adjective 6	
Adjective ending in -est	

ENRICHMENT

DAY 30 — Fill-in-the-blank story

Fill in the blanks with the words you chose on the previous page. Then read your story out loud!

Yesterday was so _____! Our family went to the beach. Before
           adjective 1

we left, we packed _____ and lots of _____.
           plural noun 1   *plural noun 2*

Once we arrived, I felt so _____. I stepped barefoot onto the
           feeling

_____ sand and saw _____ everywhere. The
adjective 2   *plural noun 3*

first thing we did was to was build a(n) _____ sandcastle with a(n)
                                  adjective 3

_____ on top. The _____ water was calling our
noun   *color*

names, so we decided to take a dip. It was so _____ and felt
                                              adjective 4

_____ on our skin. We _____, pretending to be
adjective 5   *past-tense verb*

_____. For lunch, I had a delicious _____ and
plural animal   *food*

gulped it down with a nice cold _____. After eating, we napped
                                 drink

under the _____ sky. It was the _____ day ever!
           adjective 6   *adjective ending in -est*

Weeks 7–9: Overview

Week 7

Math
Multiplying by 2
Multiplication word problems

Language arts
Sensory details
Diphthongs: oi, oy, ou, ow
Suffixes

Science
Classify animals

Enrichment
Skip-counting patterns
Finish the drawings

Week 8

Math
Multiplying by 3
Multiplication fact fluency

Language arts
Linking words
Problem and solution
Irregular past tense verbs

Social studies
Continents and oceans

Enrichment
Crack the code
Logic puzzle

Week 9

Math
Picture graphs
Multiplying by 4

Language Arts
Homophones
Vowel sounds
Combining sentences

Science
Life cycle of a plant

Enrichment
Word puzzles
Complete the pictures

More ways to learn

Keep the learning going! Use these simple, exciting activities to help you stay active, curious, and creative during your summer break.

See how many activities you can do! Cross off each activity as you complete it.

Play miniature golf and keep score.	Make a collage using old magazines.	Complete a jigsaw puzzle.
Create an obstacle course.	Make a list of things you are thankful for.	Play a card game with some friends or family members.
Make a self-portrait.	Build a fort with pillows and blankets.	Learn the words to a new song by heart.

DAY 31: Multiplying by 2

Skip count by 2s, starting at 2. Write the missing numbers.

| 2 | 4 | | | | | | | | |

You can skip count to multiply! Fill in the blanks.

Find 3 × 2. Skip count by 2s. Count 3 times.

__2__, __4__, __6__

3 × 2 = __6__

Find 4 × 2. Skip count by 2s. Count 4 times.

_____, _____, _____, _____

4 × 2 = _____

Find 7 × 2. Skip count by 2s. Count 7 times.

_____, _____, _____, _____, _____, _____, _____

7 × 2 = _____

Multiply. Use skip counting to help you.

4 × 2 = _____   6 × 2 = _____

1 × 2 = _____   3 × 2 = _____

2 × 2 = _____   5 × 2 = _____

10 × 2 = _____   8 × 2 = _____

7 × 2 = _____   9 × 2 = _____

DAY 31: Sensory details

IXL.com skill ID **8RS**

Sensory details are clues about what a character **sees**, **hears**, **smells**, **tastes**, or **feels**.

Read the story and look for the sensory details. Then complete the table.

S'more Time

I watch the fireflies light up under the trees. The smell of smoke drifts from the campfire. Insects sing, their songs mixing with the quiet noise of campers.

"Ready for s'mores?" Dad asks.

I nod with excitement. We use long sticks to roast marshmallows over the fire. Dad's marshmallow catches fire, filling the air with the scent of burning sugar. When my marshmallow turns golden brown, I pull it away from the flames. My mouth waters as I bite into the toasty marshmallow and creamy chocolate between two sweet graham crackers.

I wipe my sticky hands on my shorts and look up. A shooting star flashes across the sky! A cool breeze floats across my skin, and I pull my scratchy blanket over my legs. I close my eyes and smile. *This is the most perfect camping trip!*

	Detail 1	Detail 2
Sight	fireflies light up	
Sound		
Smell		
Taste		
Touch		

LANGUAGE ARTS

DAY 32: Multiplying by 2

IXL.com skill ID **94M**

Multiply.

3 × 2 = _____

2 × 2 = _____

1 × 2 = _____

5 × 2 = _____

8 × 2 = _____

10 × 2 = _____

4 × 2 = _____

6 × 2 = _____

7 × 2 = _____

9 × 2 = _____

Write each missing number.

_____ × 2 = 4

_____ × 2 = 16

_____ × 2 = 10

_____ × 2 = 6

_____ × 2 = 8

_____ × 2 = 18

_____ × 2 = 20

_____ × 2 = 14

_____ × 2 = 2

_____ × 2 = 12

Brain Break! Lie on your back with your hand on your stomach. Take five deep breaths. Feel your stomach rise and fall as you inhale and exhale.

DAY 32
Diphthongs: oi, oy, ou, ow

IXL.com skill ID **AGT**

Write the missing letters to complete the words. Each pair of letters will be used more than once.

> oi oy ou ow

The **b o y** raced his bike down the hill.

The old book had a **b r __ __ n** cover.

Would you like to **j __ __ n** us for lunch?

After a long day, Aashi sank into the cozy **c __ __ c h** with a sigh.

The **t __ __** robot lit up and walked across the floor.

He made the **c h __ __ c e** to bring a raincoat on a cloudy day.

The moon looked perfectly **r __ __ n d** in the night sky.

Mateo, will you add some more **s __ __ l** before you plant the seeds?

They sat **d __ __ n** for a picnic by the river.

Leo and Tara jumped for **j __ __** when their aunt surprised them at school.

74 © IXL Learning

LANGUAGE ARTS

DAY 33 — Classify animals

IXL.com skill ID **BX5**

Animals can be grouped based on traits they have in common. **Birds**, **mammals**, **fish**, **reptiles**, and **amphibians** are groups of animals.

Use the animal groups in the word bank to complete the sentences.

| birds | mammals | fish | reptiles | ~~amphibians~~ |

__Amphibians__ have moist skin and begin their lives in water.

_____ live underwater. They have fins, not limbs.

_____ have hair or fur and feed milk to their young.

_____ have scaly, waterproof skin. Most live on land.

_____ have feathers, two wings, and a beak.

Look at each picture. Then write the animal group.

roe deer

sparrowhawk

marlin

grass snake

chipmunk

fire salamander

SCIENCE

75

© IXL Learning

Day 33: Descriptive details

Adding details to your sentences can make your writing clearer and more fun to read. Here are a few kinds of descriptive details you can add:

- What something is made of or what kind it is
- Where something or someone is located
- What someone is thinking or feeling
- How something looks, smells, sounds, feels, or tastes

Add descriptive details to each sentence. Write your new sentences on the lines.

Lucas rode his bike. *Lucas happily rode his new red bike around the block.*

We made pie. _____

Look at that kite. _____

Bella hangs her painting. _____

The puppies play. _____

Marcy ate popcorn at the game. _____

DAY 34: Suffixes

A **suffix** can be added to the end of a word. It changes the meaning of the word.

Suffix	Meaning	Example
-less	without	Hope**less** means *without hope*.
-ful	full of	Joy**ful** means *full of joy*.
-ness	the state of being	Fresh**ness** means *the state of being fresh*.
-ly	in a certain way	Quick**ly** means *in a quick way*.
-ment	the action or result of	Enjoy**ment** means *the result of enjoying*.
-able	able to be	Read**able** means *able to be read*.

Circle the correct meaning of each word.

helpful	without help	full of help
happily	in a happy way	without being happy
careless	without care	full of care
believable	full of belief	able to be believed
shyness	the state of being shy	in a shy way
excitement	the result of being excited	in an excited way

Write another word you know that uses one of the suffixes above. Include the meaning of the word.

Word: _____   Meaning: _____

DAY 34 Word problems

Fill in the blanks to answer each question.

Ms. Johnson buys 3 pairs of socks. How many socks are there in all?

_____ × _____ = _____

_____ socks

Mason buys 3 boxes of donuts. Each box has 6 donuts in it. How many total donuts are there?

_____ × _____ = _____

_____ donuts

Mr. Costa ties 3 bundles of balloons to his fence for a party. There are 5 balloons in each bundle. How many balloons are there in all?

_____ × _____ = _____

_____ balloons

Jing has 3 bookshelves. Each shelf has 10 books on it. How many total books are on the bookshelves?

_____ × _____ = _____

_____ books

DAY 35

Skip-counting patterns

Complete each skip-counting pattern.

Start at 5. Count by 5s.

START FINISH

5	40	45	80
10	35	50	75
15	30	55	
20	25		

Start at 10. Count by 2s.

FINISH

	36		40
32			26
	20		
	14	12	10

START

Start at 20. Count by 4s.

START

20	24	28	
	44		
52			
80			68

FINISH

Start at 12. Count by 3s.

		24	
51	42		18
		30	15
57			12

FINISH START

DAY 35: Finish the drawings

Use your imagination to finish each drawing!

DAY 36 Linking words

IXL.com skill ID **YJC**

Linking words show how ideas go together. Look at some examples below.

Order of events	first, next, afterward, before, finally, while
Cause and effect	because, since, so, therefore, as a result
New idea or example	also, for example, in addition
Something different or surprising	or, but, even though, however

Complete each paragraph with linking words from the table.

A butterfly garden is easy to make. _____First_____, think about where your garden will be. A corner of the yard is a good place. If you don't have a yard, pots or hanging baskets work just as well. Butterflies need heat to fly, _____ pick a sunny spot. Plant bright flowers _____ butterflies like color. _____, sit back, wait, and watch for beautiful visitors.

Part of being a good friend is being a good listener. It's important to be a good listener _____ it helps our friends know we care. There are some things we can do to let our friends know we are listening. _____, we can wait for a friend to finish talking before we speak. _____, we can ask a question if we don't understand. _____ being a good listener can be hard, it helps our friends know they are important to us.

DAY 36: Multiplying by 3

Skip count by 3s, starting at 3. Write the missing numbers.

| 3 | | | | | | | | | |

Skip count to multiply. Fill in the blanks.

Find 4 × 3. Skip count by 3s. Count 4 times.

_____, _____, _____, _____

4 × 3 = _____

Find 6 × 3. Skip count by 3s. Count 6 times.

_____, _____, _____, _____, _____, _____

6 × 3 = _____

Find 8 × 3. Skip count by 3s. Count 8 times.

_____, _____, _____, _____, _____, _____, _____, _____

8 × 3 = _____

Multiply. Use skip counting to help you.

2 × 3 = _____   5 × 3 = _____

8 × 3 = _____   3 × 3 = _____

1 × 3 = _____   9 × 3 = _____

7 × 3 = _____   6 × 3 = _____

10 × 3 = _____   4 × 3 = _____

DAY 37: Problem and solution

Read the passages and write the problems and solutions in the boxes below.

A zoologist is a person who studies animals. Zoologists watch how animals live and what they do. But when people are nearby, animals may act differently. So zoologists need to be able to watch animals from far away. To do this, they use special cameras that turn on when the cameras see movement. These cameras help zoologists watch the animals without bothering them.

Problem	Solution

Seattle is a city between two large bodies of water. The city was founded in the 1800s. At that time, most of the buildings were made of wood. Heavy rains or high tides would sometimes flood the buildings and streets. Then in 1889, there was a terrible fire. It quickly burned down most of Seattle's buildings. After the fire, the people of Seattle decided to rebuild with bricks, steel, and stone so the buildings could not burn again. The people also made the new streets higher so they would not flood as often.

Problem	Solution

Multiplying by 3

Multiply.

3 × 3 = _____

5 × 3 = _____

10 × 3 = _____

6 × 3 = _____

2 × 3 = _____

7 × 3 = _____

4 × 3 = _____

9 × 3 = _____

8 × 3 = _____

Write each missing number.

_____ × 3 = 3

_____ × 3 = 18

_____ × 3 = 21

_____ × 3 = 27

_____ × 3 = 9

_____ × 3 = 30

_____ × 3 = 15

_____ × 3 = 24

_____ × 3 = 12

Get 20% off when you join IXL today!
Scan the QR code for details.

DAY 38: Consonant sounds

The letters **c** and **g** both make hard and soft sounds.

Color the words using the key.

RED	GREEN	YELLOW	BLUE
soft c sound as in **rice**	hard c sound as in **cat**	soft g sound as in **stage**	hard g sound as in **go**

gate	cent	ice	game
face	gem	page	nice
place	large	giant	city
green	bounce	space	grew
clean	camp	care	calf
group	crowd	could	glass

DAY 38: Continents and oceans

IXL.com skill ID **Z7W**

A **continent** is one of the seven largest areas of land on Earth. An **ocean** is one of the five largest bodies of salt water that cover most of the Earth's surface.

Write the names of the missing continents and oceans. Use the clues at the bottom to help you.

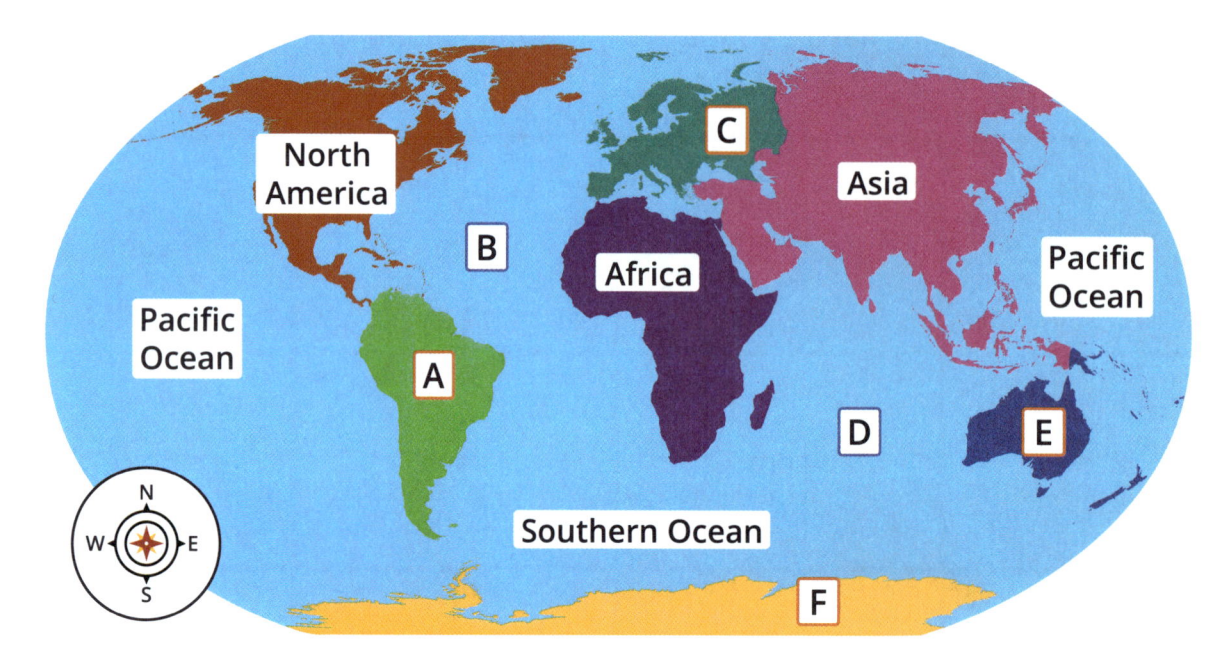

A. _____

B. _____

C. _____

D. _____

E. _____

F. _____

- **Antarctica** is a continent south of the Southern Ocean.
- The **Atlantic Ocean** is an ocean east of North America.
- **Australia** is a continent south of Asia.
- The **Indian Ocean** is an ocean east of Africa.
- **South America** is a continent south of North America.
- **Europe** is a continent north of Africa.

DAY 39: Irregular past tense

IXL.com skill ID **G88**

Fill in the blanks. Write the verb in past tense.

My friend Joel _____*rode*_____ his mountain bike on a new trail with his dad.
　　　　　　　　　　ride

Zack _____ a movie about elephants last week.
　　　　　　see

Sara _____ a picture of two colorful parrots.
　　　　　　draw

The cute dog _____ under the tree all afternoon.
　　　　　　　　sleep

Last night, Nora _____ sugar cookies with her sister.
　　　　　　　　　　make

Five ducklings _____ in a line behind their mother.
　　　　　　　　swim

During last night's storm, the wind _____ over our trash cans.
　　　　　　　　　　　　　　　　　　　blow

Write a sentence using the past-tense form of each verb.

know	
go	
are	

Brain Break! Set a timer for three minutes and doodle on a separate piece of paper or a whiteboard.

LANGUAGE ARTS

DAY 39: Multiplying by 2 and 3

Match each expression to its value.

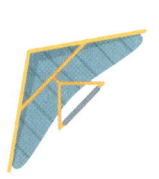

4 × 2   14

3 × 3   9

5 × 3   18

10 × 2   24

6 × 3   8

2 × 2   12

7 × 2   4

8 × 2   20

8 × 3   16

5 × 2   15

4 × 3   27

9 × 3   10

DAY 40

Crack the code

Can you crack the code? Use the picture clues to help.

Puzzle 1: ⭐ 🪺 🐜 🍦 🍋 ⭐ → **S N A I L S**

Puzzle 2: 🍒 🐜 🪺 → **C A N**

Puzzle 3: ⭐ 🍋 🐘 🐘 🍍 → **S L E E P**

Puzzle 4: 🌻 🐙 🌈 → **F O R**

Puzzle 5: 🌳 🏠 🌈 🐘 🐘 → **T H R E E**

Puzzle 6: 🪀 🐘 🐜 🌈 ⭐ 🎉 → **Y E A R S !**

Picture clues

A	B	C	D	E	F	G	H	I
ant	butterfly	cherry	duck	elephant	sunflower	gift	house	ice cream

J	K	L	M	N	O	P	Q	R
jeans	kite	lemon	mushroom	nest	octopus	pineapple	quilt	rainbow

S	T	U	V	W	X	Y	Z	!
star	tree	umbrella	violin	wheel	xylophone	yoyo	zebra	party hat

DAY 40

Logic puzzle

Sam, Caden, Asher, Maddy, and Elena meet at the park for a picnic. Each friend brings a different food to share.

Use the clues and the grid to find out which food each friend brings to the picnic.

- Maddy and Caden each bring a type of salad to the picnic.
- The person whose name comes first in the alphabet brings pasta salad.
- Maddy puts three different types of berries in her dish.
- Sam brings a dish without fruit.

	Wraps	Fruit salad	Pasta salad	Green salad	Cherry pie
Sam					
Caden					
Asher					
Maddy					
Elena					

Use your answers from the grid to finish the sentences.

Sam brings the _____.

Caden brings the _____.

Asher brings the _____.

Maddy brings the _____.

Elena brings the _____.

DAY 41: Picture graphs

The Chen, Ali, Williams, and Perez families went strawberry picking. The picture graph shows the number of baskets each family filled with strawberries.

Baskets filled

Chen family	🧺 🧺 🧺
Ali family	🧺 🧺 🧺 🧺 🧺 🧺 🧺
Williams family	🧺 🧺 🧺 🧺 🧺 🧺
Perez family	🧺 🧺

Each 🧺 = 1 basket

Answer each question.

How many baskets did the Williams family fill? _____ baskets

Which family filled the fewest baskets? _____

How many more baskets did the Ali family fill than the Chen family? _____ more baskets

How many total baskets did the families fill? _____ baskets

Brain Break! Try patting your head and rubbing your stomach at the same time. Then try swapping hands!

DAY 41 Homophones

IXL.com skill ID **Q92**

Choose the correct homophone in each sentence. Circle your answer.

These cupcakes are for | four Sabai's picnic.

My little cousin read | red three books about fire trucks at the library.

This weekend, let's try the knew | new slide at the water park!

Is this the right | write way to get to the dock?

Charlotte road | rode the train from New York City to Philadelphia.

It took about too | two years for my pineapple plant to grow just one pineapple!

Hunter walked threw | through the gate to get to his friend's house.

The farmer will way | weigh the baskets of berries for Claire and Silas.

The turtle hid inside its | it's shell when we got too close.

The birds flapped their | they're wings and soared into the clear blue sky.

Draw a picture for each homophone.

flour	flower

DAY 42 Word problems

Fill in the blanks to answer each question.

Lucia sees 4 crabs at the beach. Each crab has 2 claws. How many total claws are there?

_____ × _____ = _____

_____ claws

Mr. Clark plants 4 rectangular pots. He puts 3 plants in each pot. How many plants are there in all?

_____ × _____ = _____

_____ plants

Chef Lee makes eggs in 5 pans. There are 3 eggs in each pan. How many total eggs are there?

_____ × _____ = _____

_____ eggs

James sees 5 dogs at the park. Each dog has 4 legs. How many dog legs are there in all?

_____ × _____ = _____

_____ dog legs

MATH

DAY 42 Vowel sounds

IXL.com skill ID **8WJ**

Match the words with the same vowel sound and vowel sound spelling.

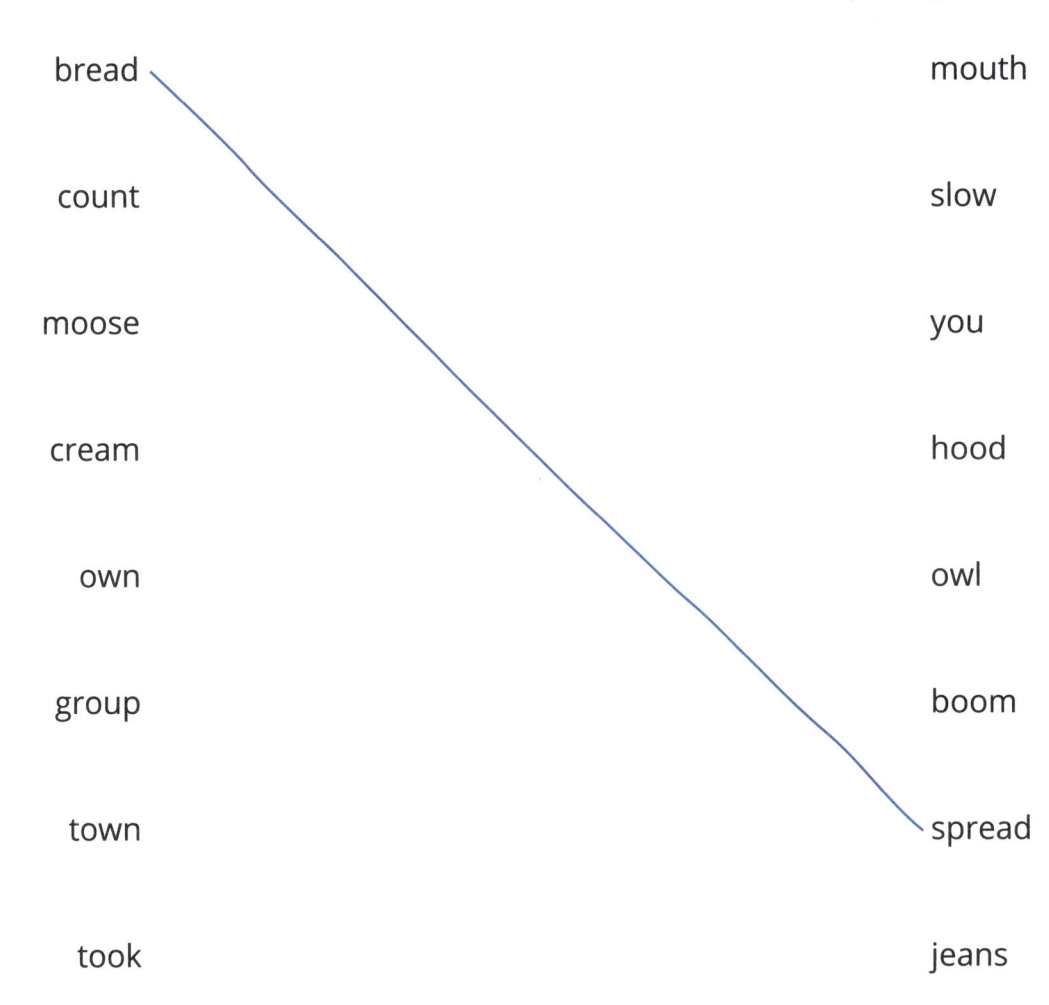

bread — spread

count

moose — boom

cream

own

group

town

took

Cross out the word in each row that has a different vowel sound.

round	shout	~~soup~~
teach	head	feast
bowl	frown	plow
stood	tooth	shook

DAY 43 Reading comprehension

Read the story. Then answer the questions.

The Colors of Home

Lorna looked out the window and sighed at all the black, empty space. She already missed her home planet, Kiron. And it would take several more hours to get to moon camp. Tears welled up in all eight of her large, purple eyes.

"Are you okay?" a voice behind her asked. Lorna looked back at the strange-looking boy who had spoken.

"Hi, I'm Zayn," the boy said.

Lorna had never seen anyone like Zayn before. He had black hair and tan skin, and he had only two eyes! But he was smiling at her, and she didn't want to hurt his feelings.

She tried not to stare as she replied. "I miss the colors back home on Kiron," Lorna said. "At sunrise this time of year, the yellow sky turns green, and the pink sea turns orange. My family always watches it together."

"That sounds pretty," said Zayn. "I miss my planet, too. Our sky is usually blue, and so is our ocean. Will you tell me more about Kiron?"

As Lorna imagined how odd a blue sky must look, she smiled back at Zayn.

Put an X under the words that are likely true about each character.

	friendly	from Earth	homesick	not human
Lorna				
Zayn				

What is the most likely reason Lorna thinks Zayn looks strange? Write your answer below. Then go back to the story and underline the words that support your answer.

_____

_____

DAY 43 Plant life cycle

IXL.com skill ID **UML**

Zoe grows cucumber plants in her garden. Her cucumber plants will follow a **life cycle**. A plant's life cycle includes growing, making new plants, and dying.

The diagram shows a cucumber plant's life cycle. Use the word bank to label the stages.

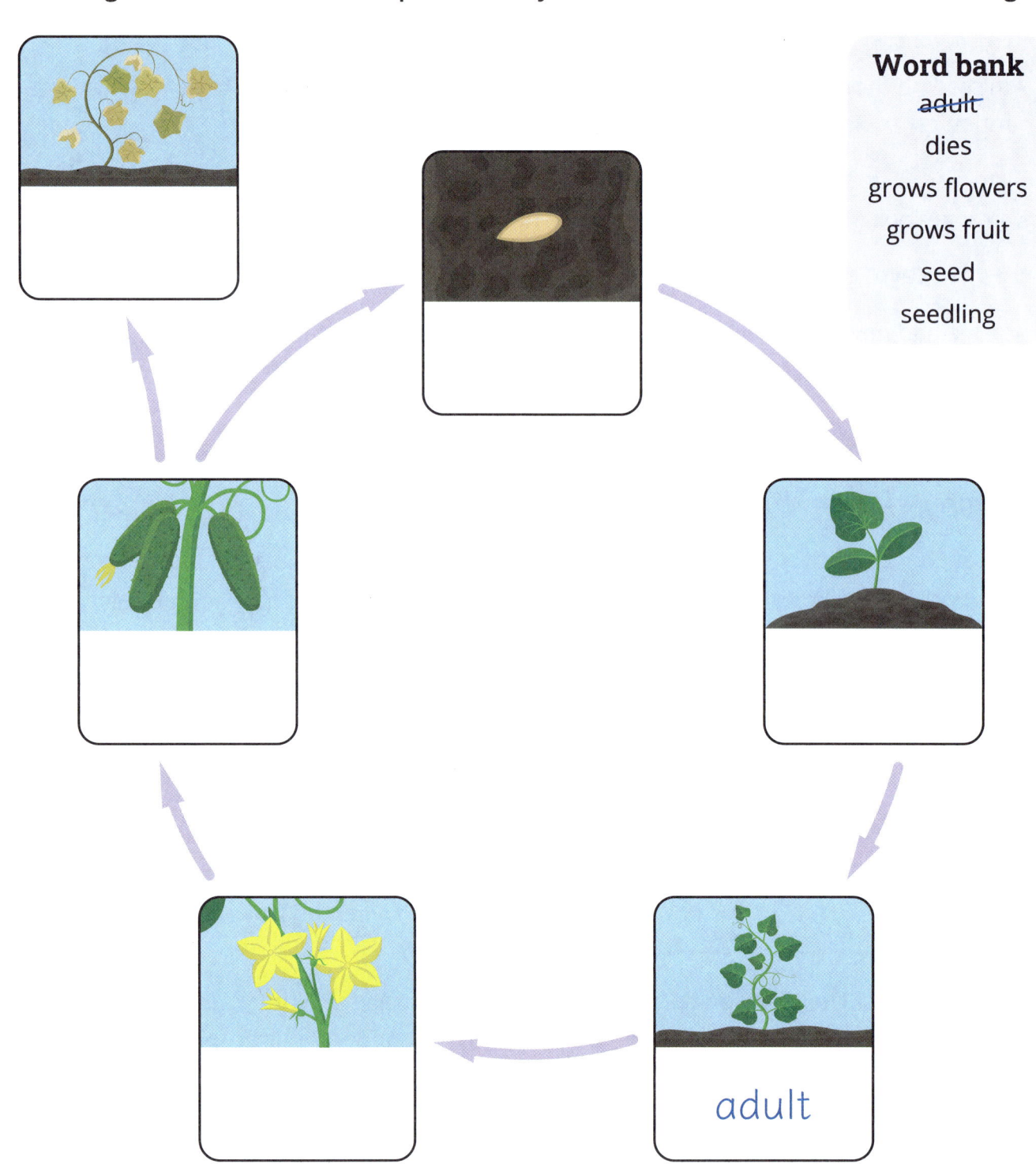

Word bank
~~adult~~
dies
grows flowers
grows fruit
seed
seedling

adult

DAY 44: Combining sentences

You can sometimes combine two short sentences to make one longer sentence. Sentences are more interesting when they have different lengths and when they don't use the same words over and over.

Combine each pair of sentences into one.

Nina loves to play tag. Andy loves to play tag.

Nina and Andy love to play tag.

Peaches are sweet. Plums are sweet.

_____

Harry paints with bright colors. Sasha paints with bright colors.

_____

Amanda went to the zoo. Amanda went to the ice cream shop.

_____

Red pandas climb. Red pandas eat bamboo.

_____

Yesterday, Tom went to the beach. Yesterday, Tom swam.

_____

DAY 44 Multiplying by 4

Skip count by 4s, starting at 4. Write the missing numbers.

Skip count to multiply. Fill in the blanks.

Find 3 × 4. Skip count by 4s. Count 3 times.

_____, _____, _____

3 × 4 = _____

Find 5 × 4. Skip count by 4s. Count 5 times.

_____, _____, _____, _____, _____

5 × 4 = _____

Find 8 × 4. Skip count by 4s. Count 8 times.

_____, _____, _____, _____, _____, _____, _____, _____

8 × 4 = _____

Multiply. Use skip counting to help you.

2 × 4 = _____   1 × 4 = _____

10 × 4 = _____   4 × 4 = _____

6 × 4 = _____   5 × 4 = _____

3 × 4 = _____   9 × 4 = _____

8 × 4 = _____   7 × 4 = _____

DAY 45 — Word puzzles

Complete each puzzle using the letters in the given word. Start with the four-letter word puzzles and then complete the six-letter ones! Each letter in the word must appear only once in each row, column, and block.

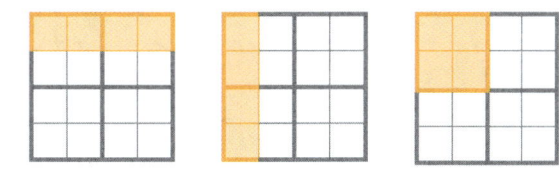

SAND

	A	N	
D	N		
N	S		A
A	D	S	N

LAKE

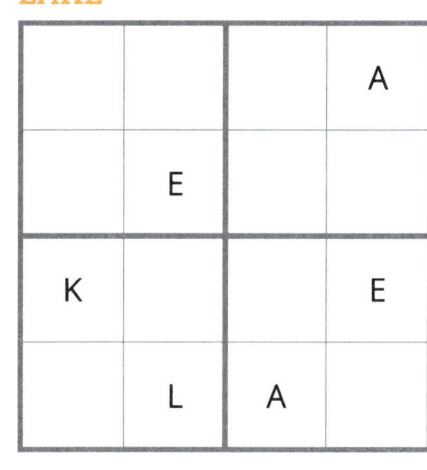

			A
		E	
K			E
	L	A	

SUNDAE

	U		N		
S		D	E		U
E			A	S	
	A		U		D
	E	N	S	U	A
		A		N	E

TRAVEL

L	T	V		E	
R	A				V
			R		
V		T	R	A	E
			L	A	
	R	A	V	E	

ENRICHMENT

DAY 45 Complete the pictures

Complete the right side of each picture so that it is a mirror image of the left side.

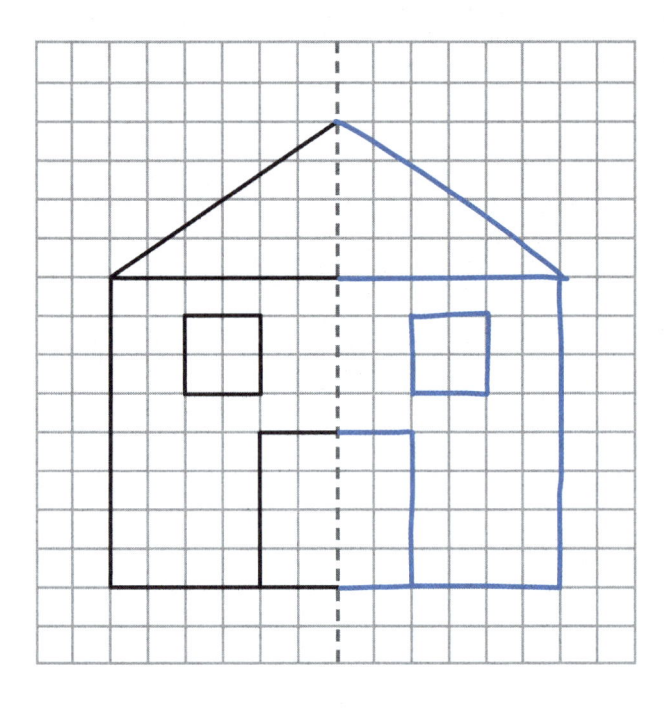

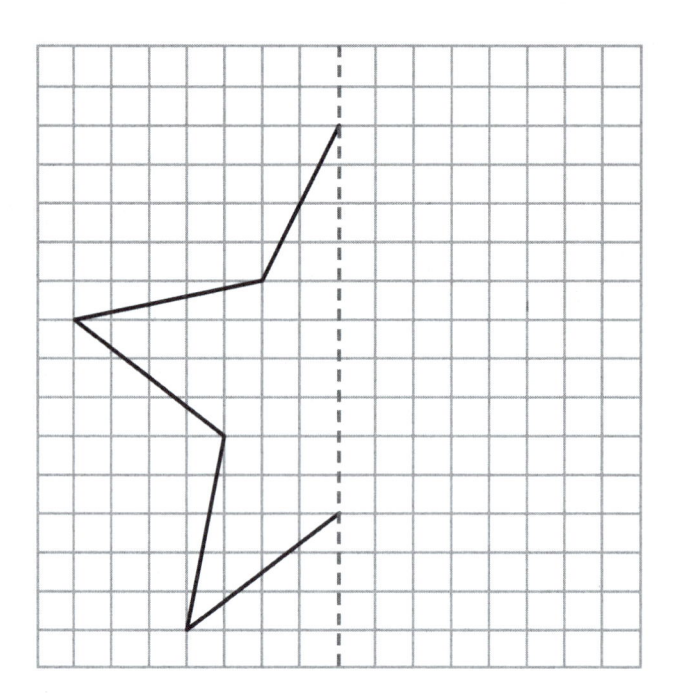

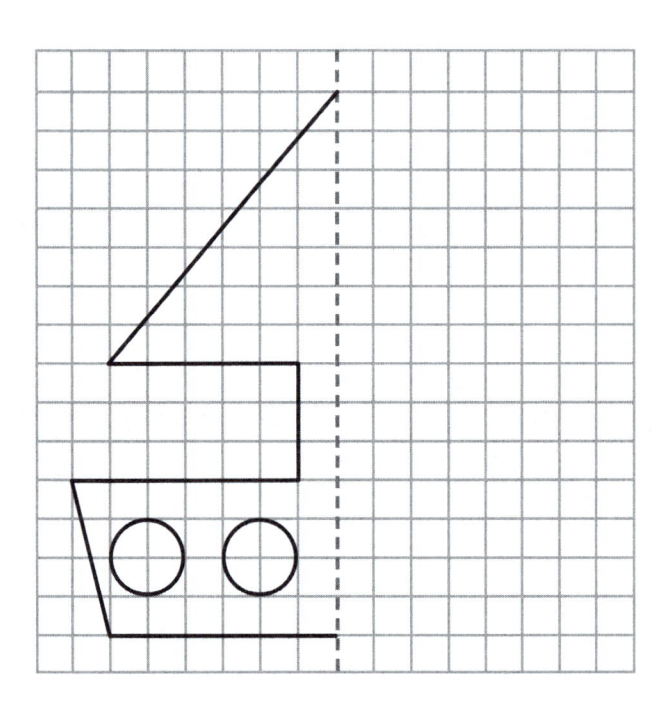

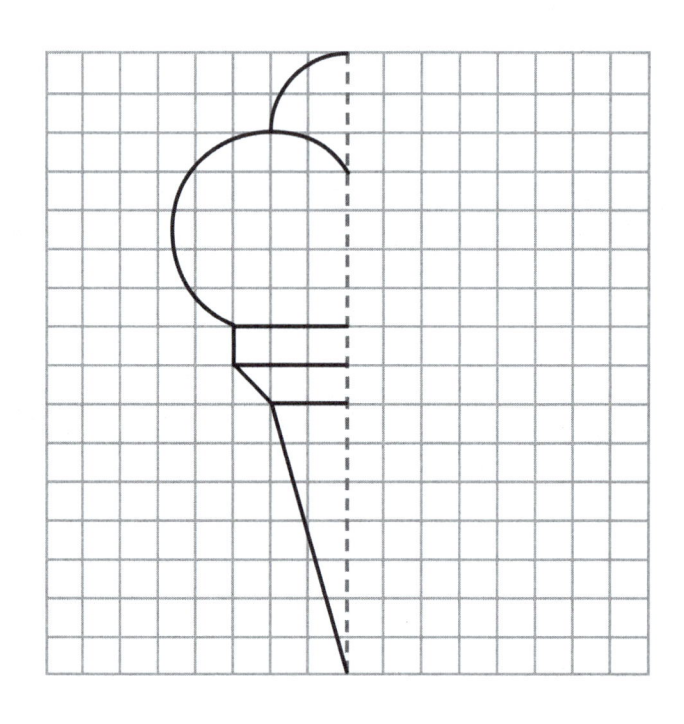

ENRICHMENT

Weeks 10–12: Overview

Week 10

Math
Multiplying by 4
Multiplying by 5

Language arts
Consonant-l-e words
Text features
Making inferences

Social studies
Jobs in the community

Enrichment
Missing number puzzles
Finish the patterns

Week 11

Math
Bar graphs
Multiplying in any order

Language arts
Possessive nouns
Understanding characters
Adding dialogue

Science
Changes to the Earth's surface

Enrichment
Math puzzles
Word building

Week 12

Math
Multiplying by 2, 3, 4, and 5
Mixed operation word problems

Language arts
Main idea and details
Nonfiction text features
Context clues

Social studies
Using a number-letter grid

Enrichment
Rhyming words tic-tac-toe
Logic puzzle

More ways to learn

Keep the learning going! Use these simple, exciting activities to help you stay active, curious, and creative during your summer break.

See how many activities you can do! Cross off each activity as you complete it.

Go on a walk and find as many different bugs as you can.	Listen to an audiobook or read a book out loud.	Set up a bean bag toss game and invite someone to play with you.
Help keep your community beautiful by cleaning up a local park.	Look up five facts about your favorite animal.	Write and illustrate a comic book.
Draw your dream bedroom and write about how it would look.	Plan a dinner menu for a week for your family.	Visit an art or science museum.

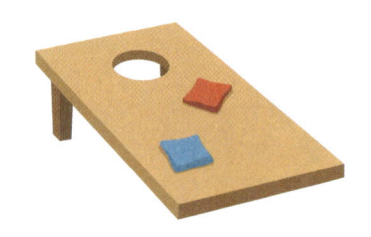

DAY 46 — Spelling consonant-l-e words

IXL.com skill ID **JGQ**

Write the word that names each picture. Each word ends in -l-e.

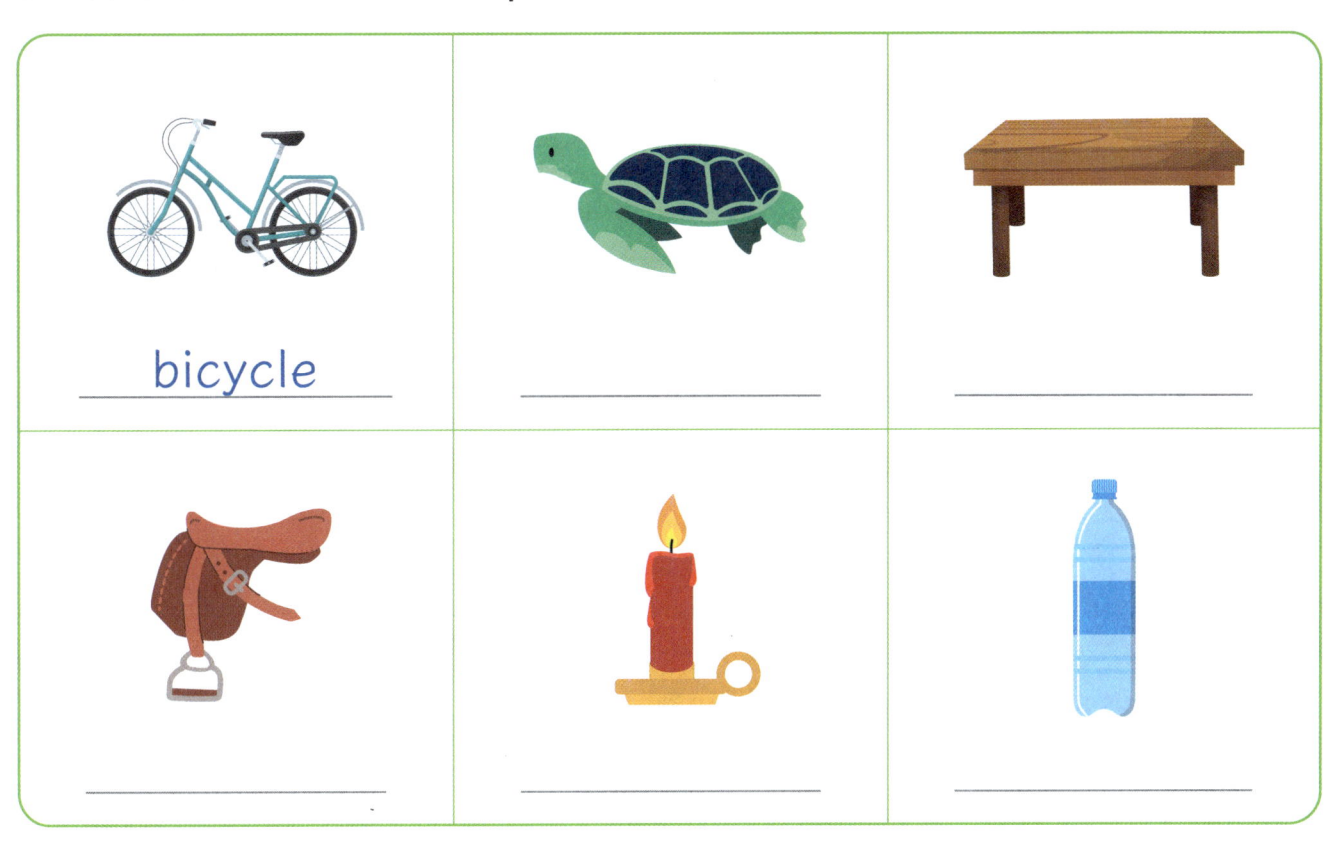

bicycle	_____	_____
_____	_____	_____

Answer each riddle with a word that ends with -l-e. Write your answers on the lines.

> whistle   puddle   puzzle   castle   buckle

What sound does a coach make when it's time to stop practice? _____

What is the metal piece on a belt called? _____

What can you splash and jump in after it rains? _____

What is a large building that has high walls and towers? _____

What has many pieces that you put together to make a picture? _____

DAY 46
Multiplying by 4

IXL.com skill ID
5U6

Multiply.

2 × 4 = _____

5 × 4 = _____

9 × 4 = _____

6 × 4 = _____

8 × 4 = _____

10 × 4 = _____

3 × 4 = _____

1 × 4 = _____

7 × 4 = _____

Write each missing number.

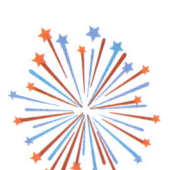

_____ × 4 = 16

_____ × 4 = 8

_____ × 4 = 32

_____ × 4 = 40

_____ × 4 = 24

_____ × 4 = 12

_____ × 4 = 28

_____ × 4 = 20

_____ × 4 = 36

Get 20% off when you join IXL today!
Scan the QR code or visit www.ixl.com/workbook/23s for details.

DAY 47 Text features

IXL.com skill ID
MKE

The following pages are from a book about fossils. Use the information on the pages to answer the questions. Write your answer on the line.

Table of Contents

What Are Fossils?	1
How They Form	3
Types of Fossils	5
Body Fossils	6
Trace Fossils	8
Casts and Molds	11
Where to Find Fossils	13
Famous Fossils	15

Which page would you turn to if you wanted to learn how fossils form? _____

You want to learn about famous fossils. Which page should you turn to? _____

On which pages would you expect to find information about trace fossils? _____

Trace fossils are fossils that show the activity of animals or plants. There are many kinds of trace fossils.

Footprints can show where animals went and how they moved.

Burrow fossils show the remains of holes or tunnels made by animals to stay safe. These fossils can tell us about how animals lived and how they might have cared for their young.

What are **two** types of trace fossils?
_____

What information can footprint fossils show?
    ____ what color animals were
    ____ how animals moved
    ____ foods animals ate

What is one thing we can learn from burrow fossils?
_____
_____

LANGUAGE ARTS

DAY 47: Multiplying by 5

Skip count by 5s, starting at 5. Write the missing numbers.

☐ ☐ ☐ ☐ ☐ ☐ ☐ ☐ ☐ ☐

Skip count to multiply. Fill in the blanks.

Find 3 × 5. Skip count by 5s. Count 3 times.

_____, _____, _____

3 × 5 = _____

Find 4 × 5. Skip count by 5s. Count 4 times.

_____, _____, _____, _____

4 × 5 = _____

Find 6 × 5. Skip count by 5s. Count 6 times.

_____, _____, _____, _____, _____, _____

6 × 5 = _____

Multiply. Use skip counting to help you.

3 × 5 = _____   6 × 5 = _____

10 × 5 = _____   1 × 5 = _____

2 × 5 = _____   4 × 5 = _____

5 × 5 = _____   8 × 5 = _____

7 × 5 = _____   9 × 5 = _____

DAY 48 — Jobs in the community

Answer each riddle. Use the jobs in the word bank.

a bus driver	a baker	a dentist
a farmer	a vet	a pilot

I work in an office. I take care of your pets. Who am I? _____

I work in a kitchen. I make bread and cakes. Who am I? _____

I work in an office. I take care of your teeth. Who am I? _____

I work in a city. I drive people where they need to go. Who am I? _____

I work in airplanes. I fly them all over the world. Who am I? _____

I work outside. I help grow the food you eat. Who am I? _____

What do you want to be when you grow up? Use the blank lines below to write a riddle about your future job.

When I grow up, I want to work in a(n) _____.
　　　　　　　　　　　　　　　　　　　place(s) where you might work

I will _____.
　　　　　　　　things you might do in this job

Who will I be? _____
　　　　　　　　　　　　　　job title

DAY 48: Making inferences

Read each part of the story and answer each question. Put an X next to the correct answer. Then underline the evidence in the text that supports your answer.

Eli sits in his seat and puts on his seat belt. He is excited to visit his Uncle Brett in Texas. Eli lives in California, so he doesn't get to see his uncle often. He looks out the window as he waits to take off. It won't be long until he's in Texas!

Where is Eli probably sitting?

____ on an airplane   ____ on a bicycle   ____ on a boat

On the first day of Eli's trip, he and Uncle Brett make a birdhouse. Eli has a hard time using the tools at first, but he learns quickly. When they finish, the birdhouse looks beautiful! Eli takes a picture of it so he can show his friends back home.

How does Eli most likely feel after building the birdhouse?

____ bored   ____ tired   ____ proud

Eli wakes up on Saturday and looks out the window. The sun is shining, and it is already pretty hot. Uncle Brett calls from the doorway, "Time to get ready, buddy! I put the chairs and umbrella in the car. Don't forget to pack a towel and swimsuit."

Where are Eli and his uncle probably going?

____ a beach   ____ a city   ____ a zoo

On Sunday, they eat dinner on the porch. As they watch the sun set, Eli sighs. He can't believe Tuesday is only two days away. He'll have to start packing tomorrow.

What is probably going to happen on Tuesday?

____ They will go camping.   ____ Eli will fly home.   ____ Uncle Brett will leave.

DAY 49: Multiplying by 5

IXL.com skill ID **Y9E**

Match each expression to its value.

2 × 5		40
10 × 5		15
3 × 5		50
6 × 5		25
1 × 5		10
5 × 5		5
7 × 5		20
4 × 5		35
8 × 5		45
9 × 5		30

(2 × 5 is matched to 10)

Brain Break! Tell a family member, pet, or stuffed animal your favorite joke!

DAY 49: Sentence variety

IXL.com skill ID **MF2**

You can make your writing more interesting when you include different kinds of sentences. One way to change a sentence is to move information from the end to the beginning.

| The car stopped <u>suddenly</u>. → <u>Suddenly</u>, the car stopped. |
| I can swim faster <u>with my goggles on</u>. → <u>With my goggles on</u>, I can swim faster. |

Write each sentence in a different way.

Jayden read his book quietly.

Quietly, Jayden read his book.

They played sports earlier today.

_____

The flowers won't grow without sunlight.

_____

The rain was falling hard when I went to bed.

_____

Enzo's family is going hiking this weekend.

_____

Ren wears a bracelet on her right arm.

_____

DAY 50

Missing number puzzles

Use the numbers 1–4 to complete each puzzle. Use each number only once.

2	×		=	8
+		–		
	×		=	3
=		=		
3		1		

	+		=	4
×		–		
	×		=	8
=		=		
4		1		

	×		=	12
–		×		
	+		=	3
=		=		
3		6		

	+		=	5
–		×		
	×		=	4
=		=		
1		12		

DAY 50

Finish the patterns

Trace and complete each pattern.

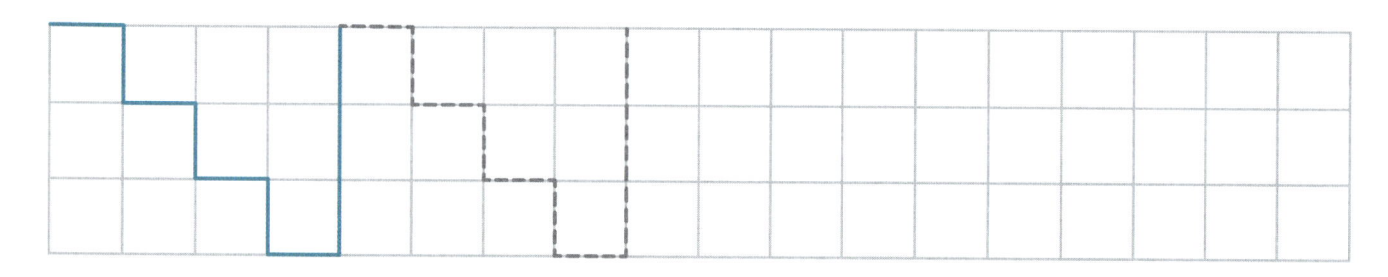

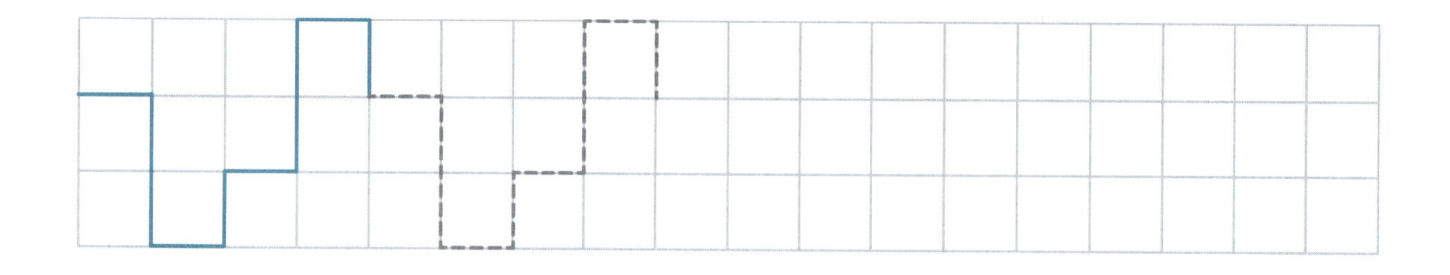

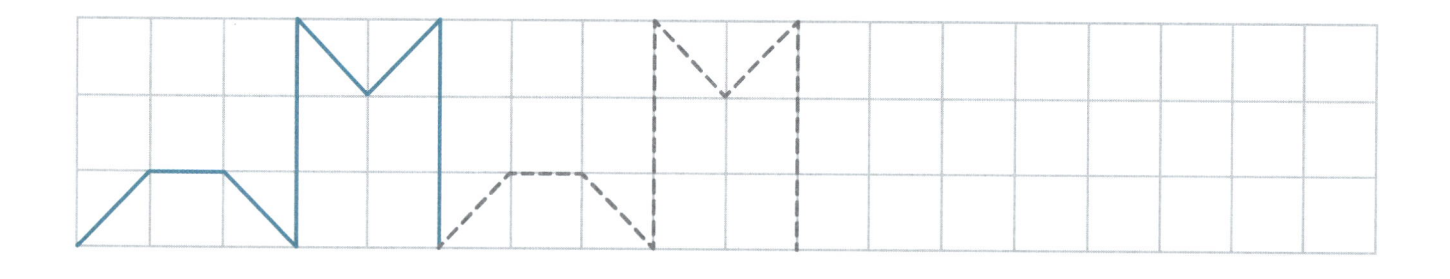

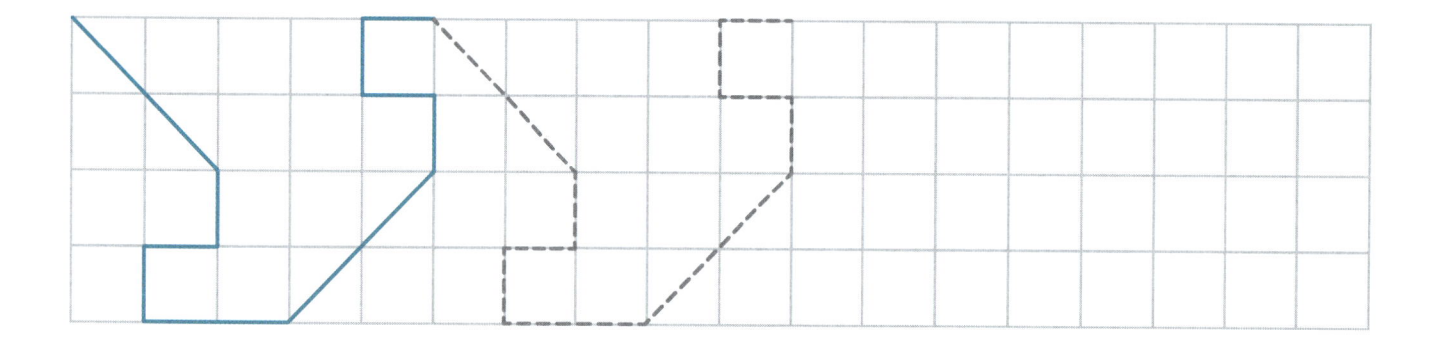

DAY 51: Bar graphs

IXL.com skill ID **8CH**

Reggie asked some of his classmates to choose their favorite summer activity. He recorded their answers on the bar graph below.

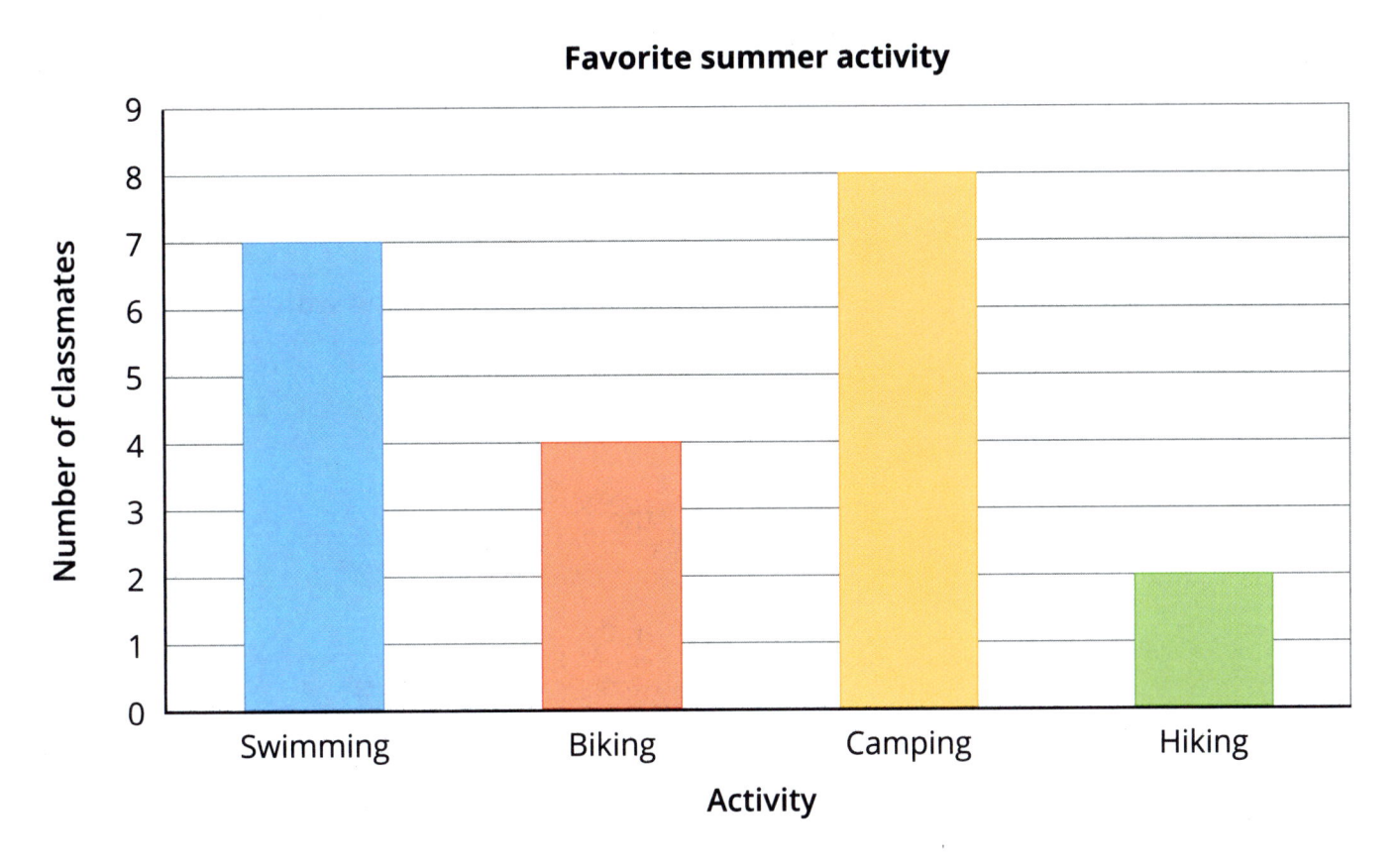

Favorite summer activity

- Swimming: 7
- Biking: 4
- Camping: 8
- Hiking: 2

Answer each question.

How many classmates chose swimming?　　　＿＿＿＿＿ classmates

Which activity is the most popular?　　　＿＿＿＿＿

How many fewer classmates chose biking than camping?　　　＿＿＿＿＿ fewer classmates

How many total classmates did Reggie ask about their favorite summer activity?　　　＿＿＿＿＿ classmates

Brain Break! Hum your favorite song and tap along to the beat!

DAY 51 Possessive nouns

IXL.com skill ID **D58**

A **possessive noun** shows who or what owns something or has something. The table below shows the rules for forming possessive nouns.

Noun	Rule	Example
Singular noun	add an apostrophe and -s	my **friend's** house
Plural noun ending in -s	add an apostrophe	the **teams'** names
Plural noun not ending in -s	add an apostrophe and -s	the **women's** shoes

Write the possessive form of the noun.

the _____**robin's**_____ nest
          robin

the _____ stems
          flowers

the _____ box
          puzzle

the _____ wool
          sheep

the _____ trunks
          elephants

the _____ shoes
          men

Fill in the blanks.

I have one hamster. Her cage is in my room.

The _____**hamster's**_____ _____**cage**_____ is in my room.

I have one neighbor. Her greenhouse is full of fruit trees.

My _____ _____ is full of fruit trees.

There are many frogs in the pond near my house. Their croaks are very loud.

The _____ _____ are very loud.

DAY 52: Multiplying in any order

Manny and Sondra each wrote multiplication equations to show the number of orange dots. Look at their work and then answer the questions.

Manny's work	Sondra's work
3 × 2 = 6	2 × 3 = 6

What is different about Manny's and Sondra's equations? What is the same? _____

_____

_____

The models above show that you can multiply in any order and get the same answer. So, if you know 6 × 2, you also know 2 × 6. Try it yourself!

2 × 8 = _____   3 × 6 = _____   4 × 10 = _____

5 × 1 = _____   5 × 7 = _____   3 × 7 = _____

2 × 9 = _____   4 × 6 = _____   4 × 9 = _____

DAY 52
Understanding characters

IXL.com skill ID **ZDC**

When you read a story, think about what the characters do and say. This can help you understand what the characters are like and how they feel.

Read the stories and answer the questions. Put an X next to the correct answers.

Dad walked up the sidewalk with five huge shopping bags in his arms. Byron peeked out the window and hurried to open the door for him.

What is Byron probably like?

_____ loud   _____ helpful   _____ messy

Annie put her hands over her ears as the music from the apartment next door got louder and louder. Her head hurt. "I wish they would turn it down," Annie moaned.

How is Annie probably feeling?

_____ cranky   _____ happy   _____ surprised

Elyse grinned at the upside-down cup on the kitchen floor. She'd caught the spider! Now all she had to do was take it outside.

What is Elyse probably like?

_____ lazy   _____ quiet   _____ brave

Greg watched the other kids talking at the snack bar, but no one talked to him. He really missed his friends back in Michigan.

How is Greg probably feeling?

_____ lonely   _____ angry   _____ hopeful

Reading comprehension

Read the story. Then answer the questions.

The Tree, the Gnome, and the Chest

In a magical forest by a peaceful river stood a young tree called Willow. One misty morning, Willow saw her friend Jerome the Gnome walking by with a wooden chest.

"Good morning, Jerome! What have you got there?" she asked, waving some of her branches toward the strange chest.

But Willow's branches were long, and they knocked the chest right out of Jerome's hands! The friends watched helplessly as the chest tumbled end over end and plopped into the river.

"Oh crumbs, there goes my chest!" said Jerome as he climbed atop a large rock. "Don't you fret, Willow, we'll get it out. We just need to use those branches of yours."

Willow carefully followed Jerome's lead as he called out directions. "A touch more left. Now down. Aha! You've got it!"

With one last big tug, Willow lifted the soaked chest from the water. Jerome smiled as he popped open the lid to check the inside. "Phew! Not a single doodad harmed. We make a wonderful team, don't you think?"

What is the main problem in this story? How do the characters solve the problem?

_____

_____

_____

What is the main theme or lesson of this story?

_____

DAY 53

Multiplying by 2, 3, 4, and 5

IXL.com skill ID **87M**

Multiply.

2 × 10 = _____   4 × 9 = _____   5 × 8 = _____

6 × 3 = _____   7 × 2 = _____   6 × 5 = _____

Fill in the blanks. Multiply the two inner numbers to get the outer number.

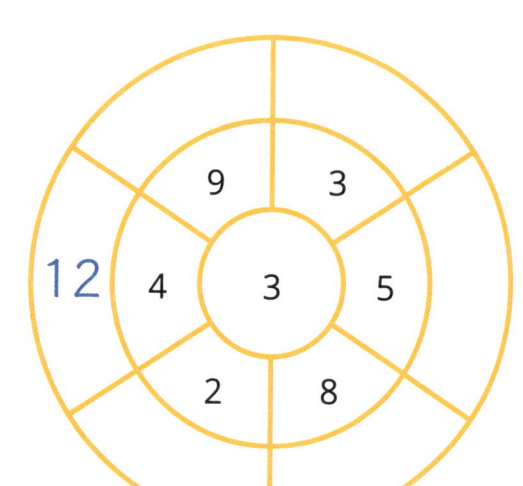

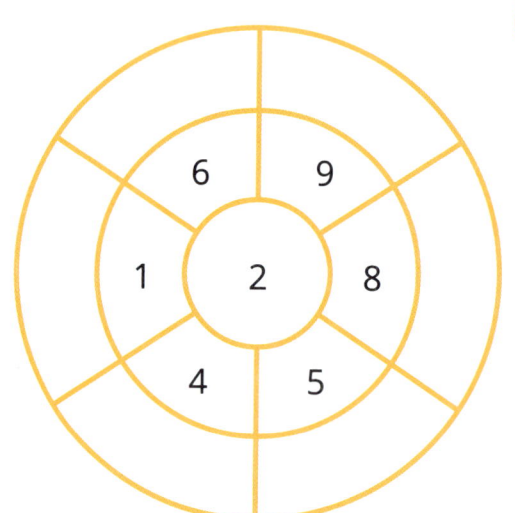

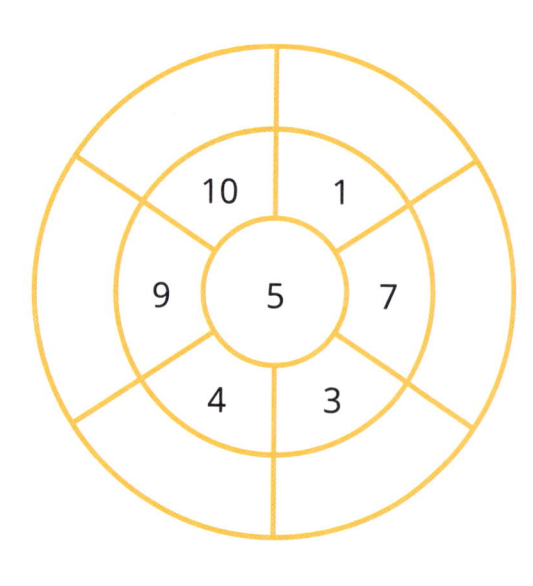

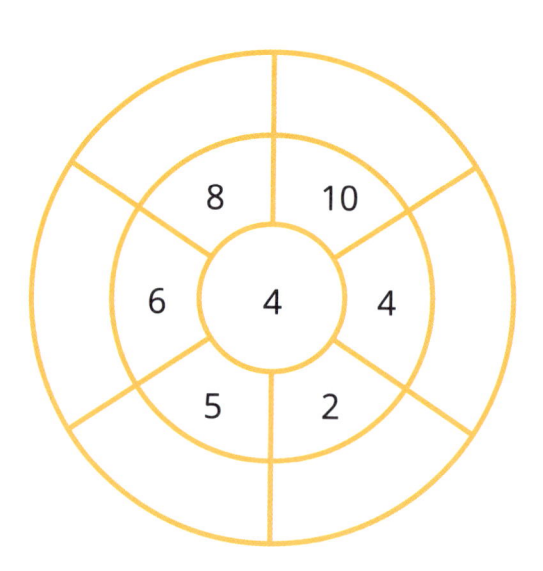

DAY 54

Changes to Earth's surface

IXL.com skill ID **XLT**

Earth's surface is covered by water and land. Even though it may seem like Earth's surface is always the same, it is always changing.

Complete the crossword puzzle. Each clue describes a change to Earth's surface. Use the clues and word bank to help you.

Word bank
landslide
flood
wildfire
volcanic eruption
erosion
drought
earthquake
deposition

Across:
3. A natural area catches fire and burns.
4. An area gets less rain or snow than usual.
6. Lava comes out from below Earth's surface.
8. Land gets covered by water after a heavy rainfall.

Down:
1. The ground in an area shakes.
2. Sand, mud, or rocks are laid down by water or wind.
5. A large amount of soil and rock quickly rolls down a hillside.
7. Water, ice, or wind causes earth and rocks to wear away.

DAY 54: Adding dialogue

IXL.com skill ID: **EHM**

Dialogue is when two or more characters in a story talk to each other. You can use dialogue to show what characters think or how they feel.

Put an X next to one choice from each section of the table. Then think about what the characters might say to each other. Write their dialogue in the speech bubbles.

Character 1: ____ A silly robot ____ A funny frog	**Character 2:** ____ A sneaky squirrel ____ A nervous dragon
Story: ____ Character 1 gives Character 2 the steps for baking a huge pizza. ____ Characters 1 and 2 plan a surprise movie night.	

Character 1   **Character 2**

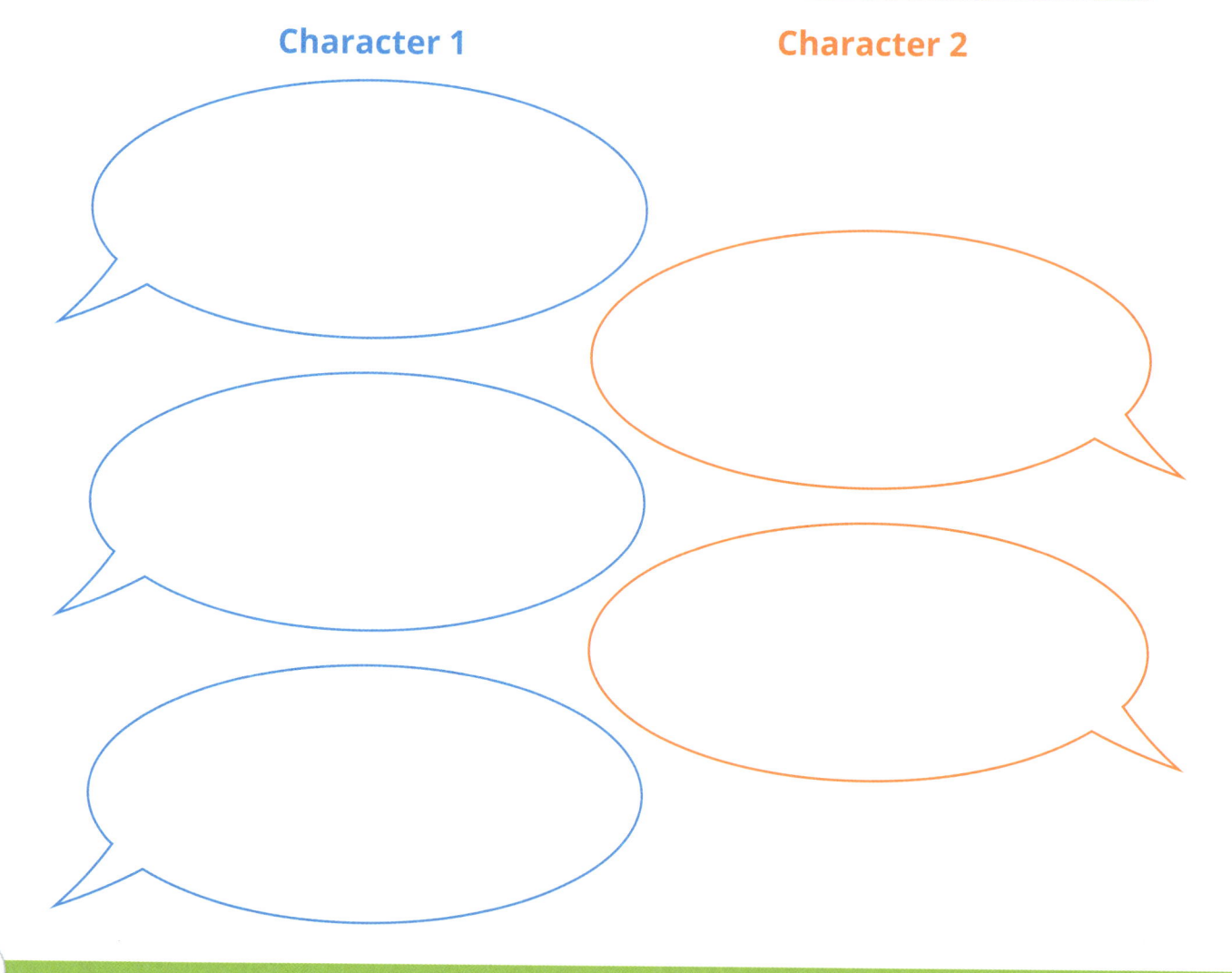

Math puzzles

Each puzzle uses the numbers 1–9 once. If you add across, you get the number on the right. If you add down, you get the number on the bottom. Fill in the missing numbers.

	7		12
9	1	6	16
		4	17
17	16	12	

1		8	13
9			21
	6		11
12	17	16	

	2		14
6			14
	7	9	17
11	14	20	

	7	6	16
2			15
		1	14
10	24	11	

	2		16
4	6		13
		8	16
10	15	20	

	1	4	10
3			19
	2		16
14	10	21	

DAY 55: Find the words

Use the letters in each phrase to make new words! For example, **summer vacation** contains the letters *s*, *e*, *a*, and *c*, which you can rearrange to make the word *case*. What other words can you find? Each word should be at least **three** letters long.

summer vacation

case

fresh watermelon

DAY 56: Main idea and details

The **main idea** of a text is the key point that the author is trying to make. It is the idea you learn from all the parts of the text together. **Details** are parts of a text that support, prove, or show the main idea.

Read each set of details. Put an X next to the main idea that ties all the details together.

Supporting details	Main idea
• Apples grow on trees. • Grapes grow on vines. • Berries grow on bushes.	____ Peaches also grow on trees. __X__ Fruit grows on different types of plants.
• People take hikes in the mountains. • Mountain streams and creeks are great places to cool off. • People look for birds in the mountains.	____ People enjoy activities in the mountains. ____ Swimming is a fun way to get cool.
• Honeybees join their legs together to help build a hive. • Some honeybees leave the hive to find flower patches. • Honeybees do a dance to show the other bees where to find flowers.	____ Honeybees need flowers to survive. ____ Honeybees work well with each other.
• The bowline knot is good for rock climbing and boating. • You can use a bowline knot to tie two ropes together. • A bowline knot can hold down a tent.	____ You can use bowline knots to stay safe outside. ____ Bowline knots can be used in many ways.

LANGUAGE ARTS

Multiplying by 2, 3, 4, and 5

IXL.com skill ID **REN**

Complete the puzzle.

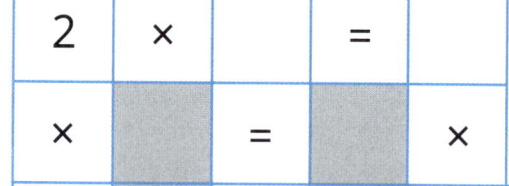

2					×	9	=			
×				×		×				
				10	×		=			
=				=		=				×
4	×	5	=			45				2
		×								=
2	×		=				×		=	12
×		=		×		×				
		25			×	7	=			
=				=		=				
	×	5	=	40		21				

Reading comprehension

Read the passage and answer the questions. Put an X next to each correct answer.

Exploring Mars

In 2003, scientists from NASA sent two rovers named *Spirit* and *Opportunity* to explore Mars. These rovers were like robots with wheels that could move around, take pictures, and send information back to Earth. *Spirit* and *Opportunity* were each about the size of a golf cart. They had cameras, tools, and long arms to study the ground. The rovers' main job was to look for signs that there was once water on Mars. Scientists were excited to learn more about the Red Planet with the help of *Spirit* and *Opportunity*.

One of the most important things the scientists discovered was that Mars once had water! The rovers found rocks and minerals that form only in wet places. This told scientists that water had flowed there in ancient times. The pictures *Spirit* and *Opportunity* sent back also showed signs that Mars likely had lakes or rivers billions of years ago. Thanks to these rovers, scientists learned much more about what Mars was like in the distant past.

What is the passage mostly about?

____ NASA   ____ Mars rovers   ____ exploring space

What is the main, or central, idea of the passage?

____ *Spirit* and *Opportunity* have helped scientists learn that there was once water on Mars.

____ *Spirit* and *Opportunity* had cameras and sent pictures back to scientists on Earth.

____ *Spirit* and *Opportunity* were sent to Mars in 2003 to look for signs that people live on the planet.

DAY 57
Use a letter-number grid

IXL.com skill ID
5ZX

A **grid** is made up of lines of squares. They are organized in rows and columns. A grid can help you use a map.

- A **row** is a line of squares that goes from side to side. Rows are marked with letters.
- A **column** is a line of squares that goes up and down. Columns are marked with numbers.

Use the map to answer the questions.

What is in row A? _____

What is in column 2? _____

What is in square B3? _____

Which square is Silver Creek Farm in? _____

What is in square C1? _____

Which squares have Fern Pond in them? _____ and _____

126 © IXL Learning   SOCIAL STUDIES

DAY 58

Word problems

IXL.com skill ID **HDU**

Rosa's family goes camping. Answer each question.

Rosa's family takes a walk by the lake. Each family member finds 5 rocks to skip. There are 5 people in Rosa's family. How many rocks do they find in all?

_____ rocks

Vincent, Rosa's older brother, makes pancakes for breakfast. He makes 5 stacks with 8 pancakes in each stack. How many pancakes does Vincent make in all?

_____ pancakes

Rosa's dad rents a canoe for 2 hours. It costs $10 each hour he rents the canoe. How much does he spend on the canoe?

_____

Rosa's family hikes 6 miles each day of the trip. The trip is 3 days long. How many miles does the family hike during the trip?

_____ miles

Rosa sees 4 deer during the trip. She takes 7 photos of each deer. How many photos of deer does Rosa take in all?

_____ photos

Brain Break! Put your hands over your heart and notice your heartbeat. Then do 20 jumping jacks. Once you finish, put your hands over your heart and notice how your heartbeat changed!

DAY 58: Multisyllabic words

IXL.com skill ID: U6F

When you read a long word, it can help to break the word into syllables. Remember, each syllable has one vowel sound. The word **cupcake** has two vowel sounds, so it has two syllables.

Say the name of each picture out loud. Circle the word that matches the picture.

needless needed needle	notebook notecard notepaper	window windmill windstorm
basement baseball basketball	robin robber robot	blueberry bluebird bluebell
pinecone pinewood pineapple	hamster hammer hamper	candy cannon canoe

DAY 59 Word problems

The city council of Spring Valley is putting on an outdoor movie night! Amir and his family attend the event. Answer each question.

A ticket for one person costs $6. Amir's family has 4 members. How much does it cost for Amir's family to enter the event?

_____

There are two screens. There are 255 families at screen A and 172 families at screen B. How many more families are at screen A than screen B?

_____ more families

The city council members sell popcorn in small, medium, and large bags. They sell 113 small bags, 96 medium bags, and 128 large bags. How many bags of popcorn do they sell in all?

_____ bags

Amir's family buys 3 small bags of popcorn for $5 each. How much money do they spend on popcorn?

_____

Screen A shows two movies, and Amir's family stays for both. The first movie is 104 minutes long. The second movie is 116 minutes long. Amir falls asleep 45 minutes before the second movie ends. How many minutes of movies does he watch before falling asleep?

_____ minutes

DAY 59: Context clues

Context clues are nearby words that help you figure out the meaning of a new word.

Use context clues to help you figure out the meaning of each bold word. Circle the answer.

My goat Missy is **bright**. She knows her name and bounces over to see me when I call her.	loud	smart	shiny
We need to walk quickly! We don't want the bus to **depart** without us.	leave	stop	beep
The **term** for the second full moon in a calendar month is a "blue moon."	week	name	band
Ruby called to **inquire** about when tennis classes begin. She wants to know more!	wonder	ask	argue
Victor wants to paint his room a new color. He hopes to **alter** his curtains, too.	change	crush	clean
We were quiet for most of the soccer match, but we **shrieked** when our team scored in the final seconds of the game.	whispered	talked	shouted

Choose one of the bold words above. Explain what clues helped you know the meaning of the word.

_____

_____

DAY 60: Rhyming words tic-tac-toe

Find the row, column, or diagonal line where all three words rhyme.

bark	cave	sharp
shark	brave	carve
walk	wave	leave

flew	fake	wake
check	knew	weak
back	cheek	threw

track	quack	quick
sack	quiet	trick
quit	sock	stick

crowd	would	cold
cloud	loud	proud
could	bold	should

through	mouse	fought
south	thought	house
brought	mouth	shout

near	teach	bears
feel	seats	each
bees	please	knees

Create your own rhyming tic-tac-toe boards! Each board should have only one answer.

Logic puzzle

The Union County Library is having a Summer Arts and Poetry Bash! There are seven children waiting in line at the face painting booth.

Use the clues to figure out the order of the line.

- Bryce is in the exact middle of the line.
- The first person's name and face paint choice start with the same letter.
- The last two people in line chose tigers.
- Elijah is directly behind Gabby.
- The second person in line chose the same face paint as the first person in line.

Name	Face paint choice
Adalyn	butterfly
Bryce	dragon
Cora	tiger
Destiny	dragon
Elijah	tiger
Finn	dragon
Gabby	butterfly

	Line order
1.	
2.	
3.	
4.	
5.	
6.	
7.	

Answer key

PAGE 7

82   56
203 802
167 941

74
423
318
890

PAGE 8

small — tiny
hop — jump
gift — present
sound — noise
unhappy — sad
beautiful — pretty
home — house
grin — smile
end — finish
stairs — steps

PAGE 9

15	18	13
6	16	8
14	8	10
19	4	17
20	16	12

8 + **4** = 12   **6** + 7 = 13   8 + **8** = 16
6 − **6** = 0   **10** + 6 = 16   13 − **9** = 4
17 − 6 = 11   3 + **12** = 15   **18** − 10 = 8
10 − 3 = 7   14 − **7** = 7   15 − **6** = 9
12 + **0** = 12   **8** + 11 = 19   20 − **10** = 10

PAGE 10

Thomas and Jake

gathering carrots

Sample answer: The character on the left is Thomas. You can tell because he's tugging a carrot out of the ground.

Sample answer: Thomas and Jake are excited. You can tell because they waited for months to taste the carrots, and they are both smiling.

PAGE 11

solid	gas	liquid
gas	liquid	solid
liquid	solid	gas

PAGE 12

C	E
E	C
E	C
C	E
E	C
C	E

Answers will vary.

PAGE 13

14 points
7 ice pops
13 times
$12
17 rocks
6 pictures

PAGE 14

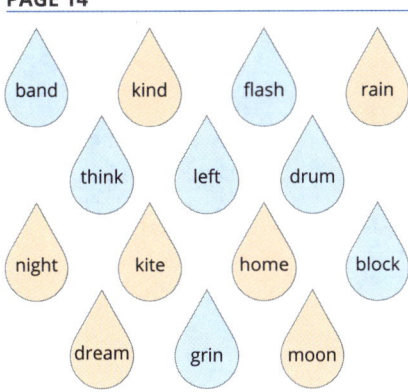

band, kind, flash, rain
think, left, drum
night, kite, home, block
dream, grin, moon

PAGE 15

2	1	**4**	3
4	3	2	1
3	**2**	1	4
1	4	3	**2**

3	4	1	2
2	1	4	3
1	2	3	4
4	3	2	1

1	3	2	4
4	2	3	1
3	1	4	2
2	**4**	1	**3**

4	1	2	3
2	3	4	**1**
3	2	1	4
1	**4**	3	2

PAGE 16

s**ail**	w**a**ve	s**a**nd
shark	**ch**air	coo**l**er
towe**l**	**gr**ill	**s**andal

Mystery word: **s**eashells

PAGE 17

gi**ft**	ne**st**	c**r**ib
de**sk**	c**l**ock	d**r**ill
string	**str**aw	**spl**ash
skunk	**pl**ant	c**r**ust

PAGE 18

11	95	64
87	18	79
5	80	22

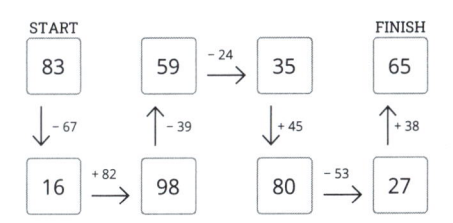

START: 83 →(−24) 59 → 35 → FINISH 65
83 ↓−67 35 ↑+38
16 →(+82) 98 →(+45) 80 →(−53) 27
16 ↑ 98 ↑−39

PAGE 19

flying squirrels

Flying squirrels have special body parts to help them get around.

soar

Sample answer: Most flying animals use wings to fly, but flying squirrels don't.

PAGE 20

| rural | urban | suburban |
| urban | suburban | rural |

Answers will vary.

PAGE 21

85 seeds
10 cucumber seeds
6 pea seeds
14 tomato seeds
75 seeds

Answer key

PAGE 22

Did anyone tell Peter that the (Game) is on (monday)?

Taylor went all the way to New (york) to see her (Aunt).

I help in the (Garden) on (tuesday) and Thursday.

Are we driving to (mount) (rushmore) in our (Tiny) car?

It's (Only) (june), but Tess knows what she wants to wear on (halloween).

My friend (maria) went on (Vacation) to Spain last (Summer).

(If) you live in Canada, you know that it snows (A) lot in (january).

My cousin (quinn's) (Birthday) (Party) is on (saturday) at the zoo.

The (Teacher) said (keenan) and (i) were the best (Swimmers) in the class.

One of my (Best) friends grew up (Here), but now (She) lives in (japan).

Answers will vary.

PAGE 23

92	75	648
560	871	329
141	759	652

94
130
752
956

PAGE 24

2
1
3

4
2
3
1

2
4
1
3

Answers will vary.

PAGE 25

A PIANO
A CLOCK
A SPONGE

PAGE 25 (continued)

RAIN
SILENCE
A BOTTLE
SHORT
YOUR NAME

PAGE 26

	Flavors			
Friends		Peach	Blackberry	Strawberry	Mint
	Ming	X	X	X	●
	Tia	●	X	X	X
	Lily	X	X	●	X
	Brody	X	●	X	X

mint

peach

strawberry

blackberry

PAGE 27

997   765   422
548   895   680
792   601   398

```
  341        597        416
+ 235      + 307      + 424
  576        904        840

  149        298        573
+ 763      + 674      + 228
  912        972        801
```

PAGE 28

Sample answer: a parade on First Street in 1929

Dottie

Sample answer: The parade is crowded, so Dottie can't see Amelia Earhart.

Sample answer: Dottie ducks under the man's arm to wave at Amelia Earhart.

PAGE 29

dirty

end

s**m**all

awak**e**

botto**m**

behind

fak**e**

ea**r**ly

Mystery word: remember

Sample answer: forget

PAGE 30

721   304   716
151   240   42
347   163   94

```
  165        944        820
-  33      - 308      - 398
  132        636        422

  934        400        702
- 527      - 156      - 596
  407        244        106
```

PAGE 31

Answers will vary. Some possible answers are shown below.

trees, flowers, dirt, rocks, bushes

A playground slide is not a natural resource. It does not come from nature. People build slides.

Water is useful because people drink water. It is also used for cleaning and bathing.

PAGE 32

ship	**b**a**th**	fi**sh**
tra**sh**	gra**ph**	**th**umb
wheel	couch	Ear**th**
chick	**ph**oto	pea**ch**

PAGE 33

12:15   9:30   4:50
7:20   8:45   1:55

PAGE 34

O   F
F   O
O   F
O   O
F   O
F   F

Answers will vary.

PAGE 35

leaf, trunk, bark

meow, oink, moo

basket, box, chest

toss, cook, crack

Answer key

PAGE 36

Answers will vary.

PAGE 39

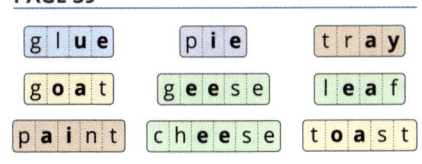

glue   pie   tray
goat   geese leaf
paint   cheese toast

PAGE 40

736 people

142 more campers

68 marshmallows

197 campers

185 boats

PAGE 41

We listened to the singer's newest song.	Michael's bright blue glasses.	Strawberries are not berries bananas are.	Most octopuses like to live alone.
Cold water on a hot afternoon.	My dog has a pile of sticks from our walks.	Forgot to bring my towel.	I love going to the lake we swim all day.
A giraffe has a long neck it can reach the leaves in tall trees.	After I found the perfect headphones for my birthday.	I baked fresh chocolate chip cookies with my sister.	The boys made a smoothie it was delicious.

PAGE 42

Producer	Consumer
Jackson	Kristen
Stella	Eric
Luna	Jason
Eliza	Carlos
Noah	Cory
Ethan	Carmen
Ashley	Seth
Ryan	Kayla

Answers will vary.

PAGE 43

5 + 5 = 10 tulips

3 + 3 + 3 = 9 towels

2 + 2 + 2 = 6 flip flops

9 + 9 = 18 chocolates

3 + 3 + 3 + 3 = 12 tennis balls

5 + 5 + 5 + 5 + 5 = 25 bananas

PAGE 44

to persuade people to come to a bake sale

PAGE 44 *(continued)*

to raise money for the Arlington Community Swim Team to travel

Arlington Community Pool

Mr. and Mrs. Fletcher

PAGE 45

E
O
R
O
E
R
R
E
O

Answers will vary.

PAGE 46

3 + 3 = 6   2 + 2 + 2 = 8

4 + 4 + 4 = 12   8 + 8 = 16

7 + 7 + 7 = 21   6 + 6 + 6 + 6 = 24

PAGE 47

Designs will vary.

PAGE 48

Answers will vary.

PAGE 49

2 + 2 + 2 = 6 slices of bread

3 groups of 2 = 6

4 + 4 = 8 eggs

2 groups of 4 = 8

5 + 5 + 5 = 15 petals

3 groups of 5 = 15

3 + 3 + 3 + 3 = 12 scoops of ice cream

4 groups of 3 = 12

PAGE 50

Answers may vary. Sample answers are shown below.

Logan is sick today.

It is raining hard.

My sister hit a home run.

Do you want to play outside?

I saw whales swimming by the boat.

Some birds fly south for the winter.

Ben should return that book to the library.

PAGE 51

Sample answer: The last shell was perfect because it fit just right and protected him from the seagull.

What you want isn't always what you need.

PAGE 52

15°C   30°C   40°F   80°F   45°C

20°C

65°F

35°F

PAGE 53

4 groups of 2 = 8

4 × 2 = 8 wheels

2 groups of 5 = 10

2 × 5 = 10 cupcakes

3 groups of 3 = 9

3 × 3 = 9 slices of lemon

4 groups of 5 = 20

4 × 5 = 20 leaves

PAGE 54

f**er**n   j**ar**   d**ir**t

y**ar**n   c**or**n   b**ur**n

sh**ar**k   sh**ir**t   st**or**m

tu**r**key   h**or**se   dess**er**t

PAGE 55

match incorrectly

use again

heat before

charge again

hear incorrectly

pay before

enter again

spell incorrectly

check before

build again

PAGE 56

sixths   halves   eighths

thirds   fourths   sixths

eighths   sixths   fourths

PAGE 57

Drawings will vary.

Answer key

PAGE 58

Answers may vary. Some sample answers are shown below.

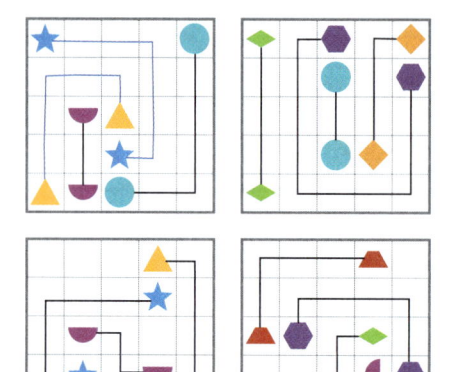

PAGE 59

Answers may vary. Some possible answers are shown below.

Both cheetahs and leopards	
• are wild cats from Africa • are fast runners and silent hunters	
Cheetahs	**Leopards**
• have round black spots • can run seventy-five miles per hour	• have open spots called rosettes • can run thirty-six miles per hour

PAGE 60

3 × 4 = 12

4 × 2 = 8

3 × 6 = 18

2 × 8 = 16

4 × 7 = 28

PAGE 61

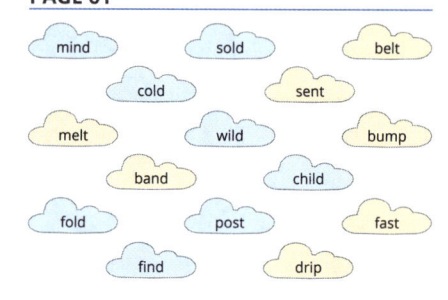

mind, sold, belt, cold, sent, melt, wild, bump, band, child, fold, post, fast, find, drip

PAGE 62

Answers may vary. Some possible answers are shown below.

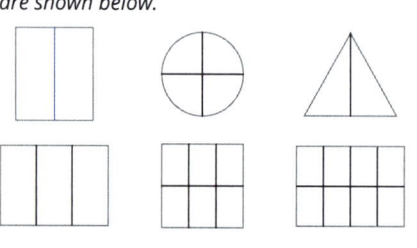

PAGE 62 (continued)

Answers may vary. Some possible answers are shown below.

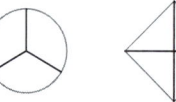

PAGE 63

The Statue of Liberty, The Lincoln Memorial, The Golden Gate Bridge

The Gateway Arch, The Washington Monument, The White House

PAGE 64

whispers

peeked

bounce

begged

crashed

plops

Answers will vary. Some possible answers are shown below.

drags

jumped, ran, dashed

race, sprint, dart

stomped, stormed, marched

banged, pounded, rapped

soar, float, drift

PAGE 65

2 × 3 = 6

6 glasses of lemonade

2 × 7 = 14

14 peas

2 × 5 = 10

10 arms

2 × 9 = 18

18 colored pencils

PAGE 66

haven't   I'm

it's   don't

we're   doesn't

didn't   you're

we'll   weren't

isn't   he'll

PAGE 66 (continued)

aren't   are not

wasn't   was not

they're   they are

she'll   she will

won't   will not

PAGE 67

Answers will vary.

PAGE 68

Answers will vary.

PAGE 71

2 4 6 8 10 12 14 16 18 20

2, 4, 6

6

2, 4, 6, 8

8

2, 4, 6, 8, 10, 12, 14

14

8   12

2   6

4   10

20   16

14   18

PAGE 72

Answers may vary. Some possible answers are shown below.

	Detail 1	Detail 2
Sight	fireflies light up	marshmallow turns golden brown
Sound	insects sing	quiet noise of campers
Smell	smell of smoke	scent of burning sugar
Taste	toasty marshmallow	creamy chocolate
Touch	sticky hands	cool breeze

PAGE 73

6   4

2   10

16   20

8   12

14   18

2 × 2 = 4   **8** × 2 = 16

5 × 2 = 10   **3** × 2 = 6

4 × 2 = 8   **9** × 2 = 18

10 × 2 = 20   **7** × 2 = 14

1 × 2 = 2   **6** × 2 = 12

136

© IXL Learning

Answer key

PAGE 74

b**oy**

br**ow**n

j**oi**n

c**ou**ch

t**oy**

ch**oi**ce

r**ou**nd

s**oi**l

d**ow**n

j**oy**

PAGE 75

Amphibians

Fish

Mammals

Reptiles

Birds

mammal　　bird　　fish

reptile　　mammal　　amphibian

PAGE 76

Answers will vary. Some possible answers are shown below.

Lucas happily rode his new red bike around the block.

We made a blueberry pie to take to the picnic on Saturday.

Look at that colorful kite dancing in the ocean breeze.

Bella proudly hangs her painting of sunflowers in the living room.

The silly brown puppies play in the backyard.

Marcy ate fresh, buttery popcorn at the baseball game last Thursday night.

PAGE 77

full of help

in a happy way

without care

able to be believed

the state of being shy

the result of being excited

Answers will vary.

PAGE 78

3 × 2 = 6

6 socks

PAGE 78 *(continued)*

3 × 6 = 18

18 donuts

3 × 5 = 15

15 balloons

3 × 10 = 30

30 books

PAGE 79

5	**40**	45	80
10	**35**	**50**	75
15	30	55	**70**
20	25	**60**	**65**

20	24	28	**32**
48	44	**40**	36
52	**56**	**60**	**64**
80	**76**	**72**	68

34	36	**38**	40
32	**30**	**28**	26
18	20	**22**	**24**
16	14	12	10

48	**45**	24	**21**
51	42	**27**	18
54	**39**	30	15
57	**36**	**33**	12

PAGE 80

Drawings will vary.

PAGE 81

Answers may vary. Some possible answers are shown below.

A butterfly garden is easy to make. **First**, think about where your garden will be. A corner of the yard is a good place. If you don't have a yard, pots or hanging baskets work just as well. Butterflies need heat to fly, **so** pick a sunny spot. Plant bright flowers **because** butterflies like color. **Finally**, sit back, wait, and watch for beautiful visitors.

Part of being a good friend is being a good listener. It's important to be a good listener **because** it helps our friends know we care. There are some things we can do to let our friends know we are listening. **For example**, we can wait for a friend to finish talking before we speak. **In addition**, we can ask a question if we don't understand. **Even though** being a good listener can be hard, it helps our friends know they are important to us.

PAGE 82

3　6　9　12　15　18　21　24　27　30

3, 6, 9, 12

12

3, 6, 9, 12, 15, 18

18

3, 6, 9, 12, 15, 18, 21, 24

24

PAGE 82 *(continued)*

6　　15

24　　9

3　　27

21　　18

30　　12

PAGE 83

Answers may vary. Some possible answers are shown below.

Problem	Solution
Zoologists need to be able to study animals without disturbing them.	Zoologists use special cameras to record what animals do without getting too close.

Problem	Solution
A fire quickly burned most of the wooden buildings.	New buildings were made of things that would not burn, such as bricks, steel, and stone.
Buildings and streets flooded when there were heavy rains or high tides.	They built the new streets higher.

PAGE 84

9　　15　　30

18　　6　　21

12　　27　　24

1 × 3 = 3　　6 × 3 = 18　　7 × 3 = 21

9 × 3 = 27　　3 × 3 = 9　　10 × 3 = 30

5 × 3 = 15　　8 × 3 = 24　　4 × 3 = 12

PAGE 85

gate	cent	ice	game
face	gem	page	nice
place	large	giant	city
green	bounce	space	grew
clean	camp	care	calf
group	crowd	could	glass

PAGE 86

A. South America　　D. Indian Ocean

B. Atlantic Ocean　　E. Australia

C. Europe　　F. Antarctica

137

© IXL Learning

Answer key

PAGE 87

rode
saw
drew
slept
made
swam
blew

Answers will vary. Some sample answers are shown below.

I **knew** it would rain today.

The Hernandez family **went** on a road trip to visit their cousins.

My sister and I **were** ready to go home after a day at the beach.

PAGE 88

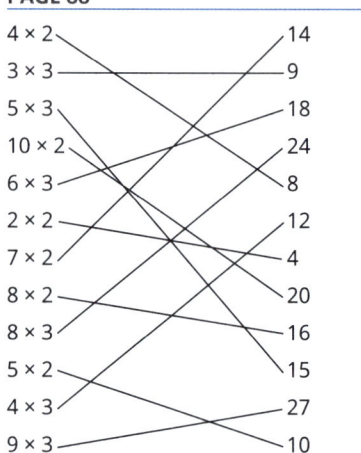

4 × 2	14
3 × 3	9
5 × 3	18
10 × 2	24
6 × 3	8
2 × 2	12
7 × 2	4
8 × 2	20
8 × 3	16
5 × 2	15
4 × 3	27
9 × 3	10

PAGE 89

Snails can
sleep for
three years!

PAGE 90

		Foods				
		Wraps	Fruit salad	Pasta salad	Green salad	Cherry pie
Friends	Sam	●	X	X	X	X
	Caden	X	X	X	●	X
	Asher	X	X	●	X	X
	Maddy	X	●	X	X	X
	Elena	X	X	X	X	●

wraps
green salad
pasta salad
fruit salad
cherry pie

PAGE 91

6 baskets
the Perez family
4 more baskets
18 baskets

PAGE 92

for
read
new
right
rode
two
through
weigh
its
their

Drawings will vary.

PAGE 93

4 × 2 = 8
8 claws

4 × 3 = 12
12 plants

5 × 3 = 15
15 eggs

5 × 4 = 20
20 dog legs

PAGE 94

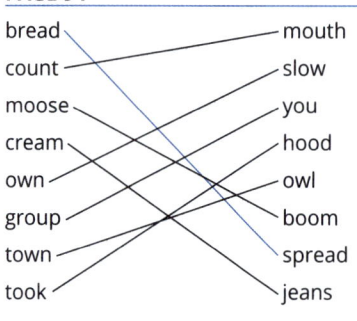

bread	mouth
count	slow
moose	you
cream	hood
own	owl
group	boom
town	spread
took	jeans

soup
head
bowl
tooth

PAGE 95

	friendly	from Earth	homesick	not human
Lorna	X		X	X
Zayn	X	X	X	

PAGE 95 *(continued)*

Sample answer: Zayn is a human, but Lorna isn't. Lorna has probably never seen a human before.

Underlined words will vary.

PAGE 96

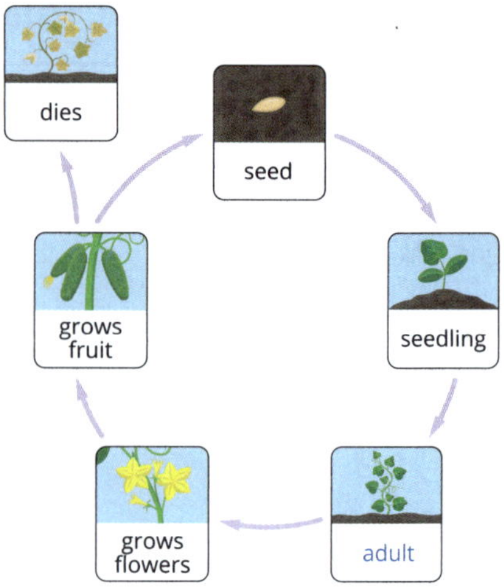

dies
seed
seedling
adult
grows flowers
grows fruit

PAGE 97

Answers may vary. Some possible answers are shown below.

Nina and Andy love to play tag.

Peaches and plums are sweet.

Harry and Sasha paint with bright colors.

Amanda went to the zoo and the ice cream shop.

Red pandas climb and eat bamboo.

Yesterday, Tom went to the beach and swam.

PAGE 98

4 8 12 16 20 24 28 32 36 40

4, 8, 12
12

4, 8, 12, 16, 20
20

4, 8, 12, 16, 20, 24, 28, 32
32

8	4
40	16
24	20
12	36
32	28

Answer key

PAGE 99

S	A	N	D
D	N	A	S
N	S	D	A
A	D	S	N

L	K	E	A
A	E	K	L
K	A	L	E
E	L	A	K

A	U	E	N	D	S
S	N	D	E	A	U
E	D	U	A	S	N
N	A	S	U	E	D
D	E	N	S	U	A
U	S	A	D	N	E

L	T	V	E	R	A
R	A	E	L	V	T
A	E	R	T	L	V
V	L	T	R	A	E
E	V	L	A	T	R
T	R	A	V	E	L

PAGE 100

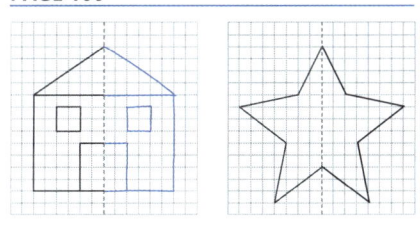

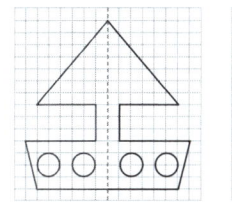

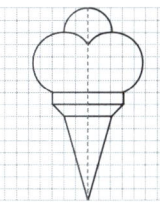

PAGE 103

| bicycle | turtle | table |
| saddle | candle | bottle |

whistle

buckle

puddle

castle

puzzle

PAGE 104

8	20	36
24	32	40
12	4	28

4 × 4 = 16	2 × 4 = 8	8 × 4 = 32
10 × 4 = 40	6 × 4 = 24	3 × 4 = 12
7 × 4 = 28	5 × 4 = 20	9 × 4 = 36

PAGE 105

page 3

page 15

pages 8–10

PAGE 105 (continued)

footprints and burrow fossils

how animals moved

Sample answer: how animals might have cared for their young

PAGE 106

5 10 15 20 25 30 35 40 45 50

5, 10, 15

15

5, 10, 15, 20

20

5, 10, 15, 20, 25, 30

30

15	30
50	5
10	20
25	40
35	45

PAGE 107

a vet

a baker

a dentist

a bus driver

a pilot

a farmer

Answers will vary.

PAGE 108

on an airplane

proud

a beach

Eli will fly home.

Underlined evidence will vary.

PAGE 109

2 × 5 — 40
10 × 5 — 15
3 × 5 — 50
6 × 5 — 25
1 × 5 — 10
5 × 5 — 5
7 × 5 — 20
4 × 5 — 35
8 × 5 — 45
9 × 5 — 30

PAGE 110

Quietly, Jayden read his book.

Earlier today, they played sports.

Without sunlight, the flowers won't grow.

When I went to bed, the rain was falling hard.

This weekend, Enzo's family is going hiking.

On her right arm, Ren wears a bracelet.

PAGE 111

2	×	4	=	8
+		−		
1	×	3	=	3
=		=		
3		1		

1	+	3	=	4
×		−		
4	×	2	=	8
=		=		
4		1		

4	×	3	=	12
−		×		
1	+	2	=	3
=		=		
3		6		

2	+	3	=	5
−		×		
1	×	4	=	4
=		=		
1		12		

PAGE 112

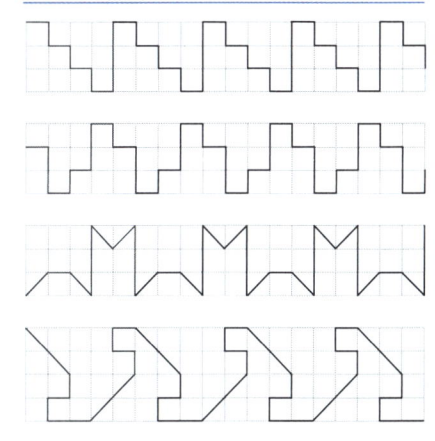

PAGE 113

7 classmates

camping

4 fewer classmates

21 classmates

139

© IXL Learning

Answer key

PAGE 114

robin's
puzzle's
elephants'

flowers'
sheep's
men's

hamster's cage
neighbor's greenhouse
frogs' croaks

PAGE 115

Sample answer: Manny's and Sondra's equations multiply the numbers 2 and 3 in a different order. Both equations have a product of 6.

16	18	40
5	35	21
18	24	36

PAGE 116

helpful
cranky
brave
lonely

PAGE 117

Sample answer: Willow accidentally knocked Jerome's chest into the river. Jerome told Willow where to guide her branches so they could get the chest back.

Sample answer: Working together is a good way to solve problems.

PAGE 118

| 20 | 36 | 40 |
| 18 | 14 | 30 |

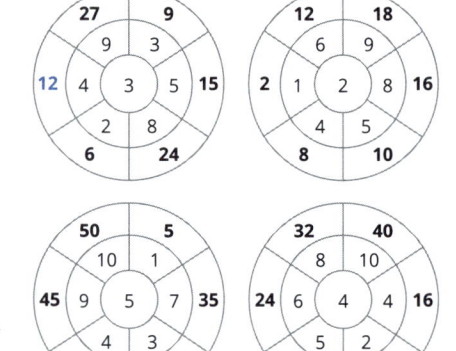

Circle 1: 27, 9, 3, 5, 8, 24, 6, 2, 4, 3, 9, 12, 15
Circle 2: 12, 18, 6, 9, 2, 1, 2, 8, 16, 4, 5, 8, 10
Circle 3: 50, 5, 10, 1, 45, 9, 5, 7, 35, 4, 3, 20, 15
Circle 4: 32, 40, 8, 10, 24, 6, 4, 4, 16, 5, 2, 20, 8

PAGE 119

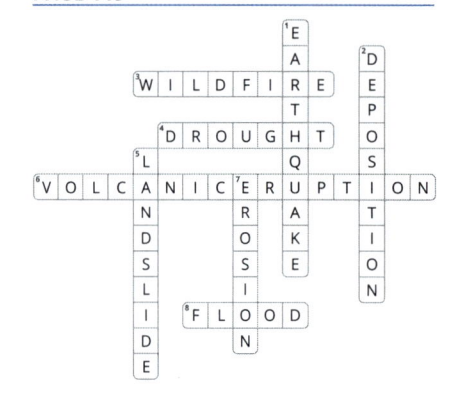

Crossword:
1. WILDFIRE
3. DEPOSIT (down) / EARTHQUAKE (down)
4. DROUGHT
5. LANDSLIDE (down)
6. VOLCANIC ERUPTION
8. FLOOD

PAGE 120

Answers will vary.

PAGE 121

3	7	2	12
9	1	6	16
5	8	4	17
17	16	12	

1	4	8	13
9	7	5	21
2	6	3	11
12	17	16	

4	2	8	14
6	5	3	14
1	7	9	17
11	14	20	

3	7	6	16
2	9	4	15
5	8	1	14
10	24	11	

5	2	9	16
4	6	3	13
1	7	8	16
10	15	20	

5	1	4	10
3	7	9	19
6	2	8	16
14	10	21	

PAGE 122

Answers will vary. Some possible answers are shown below.

case, eat, mat
net, aim, item
scan, tune, timer
stare, amuse, scream

let, her, wet
sat, man, form
melt, warm, tree
later, lemon, flame

PAGE 123

Fruit grows on different types of plants.
People enjoy activities in the mountains.
Honeybees work well with each other.
Bowline knots can be used in many ways.

PAGE 124

2		2	×	9	=	18	
×		×		×			
2		10	×	5	=	50	6
=		=		=			×
4	×	5	=	20		45	2
		×					=
2	×	5	=	10		3	×	4	=	12
×		=		×		×
4		25		4	×	7	=	28
=				=		=
8	×	5	=	40		21

PAGE 125

Mars rovers

Spirit and *Opportunity* have helped scientists learn that there was once water on Mars.

PAGE 126

Westgate Station
Sweetbriar Orchard
Hillsdale Library
D3
Honeycomb Goods
C4 and D4

PAGE 127

25 rocks
40 pancakes
$20
18 miles
28 photos

PAGE 128

needle	notebook	windmill
baseball	robot	blueberry
pineapple	hammer	canoe

PAGE 129

$24
83 more families
337 bags
$15
175 minutes

Answer key

PAGE 130

smart

leave

name

ask

change

shouted

Answers will vary.

PAGE 131

bark	cave	sharp
shark	brave	carve
walk	wave	leave

flew	fake	wake
check	knew	weak
back	cheek	threw

track	quack	quick
sack	quiet	trick
quit	sock	stick

crowd	would	cold
cloud	loud	proud
could	bold	should

through	mouse	fought
south	thought	house
brought	mouth	shout

near	teach	bears
feel	seats	each
bees	please	knees

Answers will vary.

PAGE 132

1. Destiny
2. Finn
3. Adalyn
4. Bryce
5. Gabby
6. Elijah
7. Cora

Notes

Certificate of Completion

Congratulations!

_____
Name

has completed this year's **Ultimate Summer Workbook** and is ready for grade 3!

_____
Awarded by

_____
Date